*Also by D. C. M. Platt*

FINANCE, TRADE AND POLITICS IN BRITISH FOREIGN POLICY, 1815–1914
THE CINDERELLA SERVICE: British Consuls since 1825
LATIN AMERICA AND BRITISH TRADE, 1806–1914
FOREIGN FINANCE IN CONTINENTAL EUROPE AND THE USA, 1815–1870
BUSINESS IMPERIALISM, 1840–1930: An Inquiry based on British Experience in Latin America (*editor*)
ARGENTINA, AUSTRALIA AND CANADA: Studies in Comparative Development, 1870–1965 (*editor with Guido di Tella*)
THE POLITICAL ECONOMY OF ARGENTINA, 1880–1946 (*editor with Guido di Tella*)

# BRITAIN'S INVESTMENT OVERSEAS ON THE EVE OF THE FIRST WORLD WAR

# Britain's Investment Overseas on the Eve of the First World War

## The Use and Abuse of Numbers

D. C. M. Platt

St. Martin's Press New York

Scholarly & Reference Division,
St. Martin's Press, Inc., 175 Fifth Avenue, New York, NY 10010

First published in the United States of America in 1986

Printed in Great Britain

ISBN 0–312–09673–9

Library of Congress Cataloging-in-Publication Data
Platt, D. C. M. (Desmond Christopher Martin), 1934–
Britain's investment overseas on the eve of the
First World War.
Bibliography: p.
Includes index.
1. Investments, British—History. I. Title.
HG4538.P5 1986 332.6′7341 86–6506
ISBN 0–312–09673–9

But in case you should think my education was wasted
  I hasten to explain
That having once been to the University of Oxford
  You can never really again
Believe anything that anyone says and that of course is an asset
  In a world like ours;
Why bother to water a garden
  That is planted with paper flowers?

Louis MacNeice, *Autumn Journal* (London, 1939)

# Contents

PART III IMPLICATIONS AND CONCLUSIONS

# List of Tables

# Rates of Exchange: March 1914

(£1 sterling = 20 shillings = 240 pence)

| | *Shillings* | *Pence* |
|---|---|---|
| Argentina: peso (gold) | 3 | 11 |
| Austro-Hungary: krone | | 10 |
| China: tael | 2 | 4½ |
| Egypt: £E | 20 | 6 |
| France: franc | | 9½ |
| Germany: reichsmark | | 11⅘ |
| Holland: florin or gulden | 1 | 8 |
| Italy: lira | | 9½ |
| Russia: rouble | 2 | 1½ |
| USA: dollar | 4 | 1½ |

*Source*: *Stock Exchange Official Intelligence for 1914* (London, 1914) p. 1715.

# Abbreviations

1. Sir George Paish's three papers of 1909, 1911 and 1914 appear regularly throughout the text. These are abbreviated as Paish (1909), Paish (1911) and Paish (1914). The full references are:

   'Great Britain's Capital Investments in Other Lands', *Journal of the Royal Statistical Society*, LXXII (1909) pp. 465–95.
   'Great Britain's Capital Investments in Individual Colonies and Foreign Countries', ibid., LXXIV (1911) pp. 167–200.
   'The Export of Capital and the Cost of Living', *Statist* (Supplement), 14 Feb. 1914, pp. i–viii.

2. All places of publication in footnotes can be assumed to be London unless shown otherwise.

# Preface and Acknowledgements

Benjamin Jowett, once Master of my first, Oxford, college, explained long ago that the truth was very often troublesome, but that the world could not get on without it. This book is an attempt to approach one aspect of the truth through numbers. My intention is to supply a revised, updated estimate for an important number in the economic history of Britain – British investment overseas as it stood on the eve of the First World War, at the very peak of Britain's international power. Simultaneously, I offer one example of what can happen to numbers in the study of history, what has been done with them, what they can come to imply, and what approach we may wish to adopt in future.

Many of the points that this book raises have been discussed at one time or another with my colleagues and students at this and other universities, and I am more than conventionally grateful for their comments and advice. I owe an especial debt to Professor Mira Wilkins of Florida International University and to Dr Patrick O'Brien of St Antony's College, Oxford, both of whom spent much time and care on simplifying and correcting my ideas. Dr Stanley Chapman of the University of Nottingham, Dr Ranald Michie of the University of Durham, and Professor Sidney Pollard of the University of Bielefeld have also been immensely helpful. If I may borrow Jan Morris's ingenious formula, I am grateful to all those referees for the *Economic History Review* who saw these ideas at an earlier, more primitive stage, save one . . . I must acknowledge with thanks the generosity of the Economic and Social Research Council (grant no. B00230015) for funding a research officer, Dr Rachel Whitehead, without whose assistance this book could not have been written. Mrs Carmichael and her staff at the History Faculty Office at Oxford, Miss Williams and Mrs Linton of St Antony's College, have jointly undertaken the typing of an awkward script, with much kindness and goodwill.

It is to my wife, Sylvia, that I owe the most for her patience, her sympathy and her active, professional assistance in the preparation of the typescript for publication.

*St Antony's College*
*Oxford*

D. C. M. Platt

# Part I
# Introduction

# 1 Approach and Methods

Numbers matter, and a realistic estimate of Britain's position as the prime, international lender just before the First World War matters more than most. A more professional figure has many implications for the health and shape of the economy both in Britain and abroad, and I shall suggest just a few at the end of this book. Meanwhile, I want to explain how the conventional figure of £4 billion was reached, why it has been with us for nearly three-quarters of a century, and what (within wide limits) it is now more likely to have been.

This is not simply a matter of 'method', although methods and a closer approximation to an accurate figure are important. Large numbers are often no more than symbols – they meant powerful armies in the Middle Ages just as today they confirm the 'success' of a political demonstration. In much the same way, estimates were prepared by contemporary publicists and political economists specifically to establish, by the magnitude of foreign investment, the financial strength of rival powers on the brink of the First World War. Estimates have been exchanged ever since, for which one method is thought sometimes to be better than another, and then another better still as fashion changes. In the middle of all this competitive endeavour, both economic and non-economic elements overlap. So they must for any period of history, and not least for those years before the war when great social and political change, growing competition in trade and finance, suspicion of conspiracy among both radicals and the establishment, Conservative 'Fair Traders' in furious debate with Liberal 'Free Traders', national pride and international propaganda, ended with the Powers locked in battle.

Felix Schuster, vice-president of the Institute of Bankers, while defending himself before his members in 1904 on the puzzling question of an accurate estimate for the stock of US railway securities held by Britons, made the intelligent comment that in an area for which no statistics were available 'we can judge only by the information we can gather in our business experience'.[1] Schuster had done so himself. He knew that bankers and brokers worked often by little more than instinct, fed and 'improved' by gossip, by scraps of information and by a 'feel' for the market.

It is this that has made me wonder whether we are on the right track. A run of figures, whatever the source, may contain deficiencies obvious only from contemporary business experience – the current state of the market in London for US rails, for South African 'kaffirs', for Russian state loans . . . In a recent book on the quantities and distribution of foreign investment from 1815 to 1870, I drew heavily both on the correspondence of merchant bankers and on the information available contemporaneously to brokers, specialist writers, and the financial press. The results were unexpected, and they led me to suggest a downward revision of the conventional figure for Britain's foreign investment in 1870 by as much as 50 per cent.[2] The correspondence of merchant bankers, on which so much of this revision depended, is not so readily accessible for the period from 1870 to the First World War, neither is it so especially informative within what had become a wider and more competitive market. By now, in any case, the financial press was much improved – it was more independent, better informed and more responsible. It is from brokers' intelligence and from financial journalism, much swollen by an immense volume of published pamphlets, articles and books, contemporary and modern, that I now put forward my evidence and conclusions for the 'stock' of British investment overseas in 1914. By 'stock' I mean the quantity actually held by investors resident in Britain on the eve of the First World War, both of such securities as passed through the Stock Exchange (portfolio) and of the investment placed privately without the intermediation of brokers (direct). The downvaluation, if not quite so dramatic as for 1870, is more precise and perhaps as challenging. Naturally, total investment in 1914 was much larger, Britain's economy more deeply implicated, and the consequences of downvaluation greater in influence and effect.

## DEFINITIONS

It is useful to establish from the first some simple definitions. 'Portfolio investment' has been defined as 'long-term investment in the form of marketable securities'.[3] My estimates for portfolio investment, although starting with London and the new issue market, take into account what is known as the 'secondary market' – the return of securities to the original market, resale and a change of ownership.

For 1914 I am proposing a revised stock figure of £2.63 billion for portfolio investment, together with an estimate of £500 million for the stock of 'direct' investment at the same date. 'Direct' investment, as redefined by the US Department of Commerce, has come to mean investment by firms partially controlled from abroad. The required degree of foreign ownership and control has been reduced since the 1930s, when the distinction was first made, to only 10 per cent. For the sake of simplicity and comparison, it seems sensible here to use 'direct' in the sense employed before the Great War, i.e. all capital invested privately that did not pass through a public stock exchange. Herbert Feis neatly defines direct investment as 'investment that did not leave traces in the securities markets'.

Furthermore, 'stock' figures are very different from 'flows'. 'Stock' is the sum of investment *held* on a particular date; 'flows' are the accumulation of investment year by year. Four billion pounds sterling is the 'stock' figure that we have had at the back of our minds for Britain's investment abroad on the eve of the First World War. It is taken from Sir George Paish's estimate for 31 December 1913. What if the portfolio component of this figure (£3.7 billion), even including such portfolio investment as took place subsequently up to August 1914, were very nearly 30 per cent too high?

## THE CIRCULATION OF SIR GEORGE PAISH'S DIRECT ESTIMATES

There are two basic approaches to an estimate for 1914, and I will be taking a look at both. One is the 'direct' method – the calculation of the amount of foreign securities issued on British markets, broken down by nation and by function. The other is 'indirect', designed to establish what Keynes called 'net investment', meaning the 'favourable balance of trade on income account'.[4]

The conventional, stock figure for British investment overseas came originally from George Paish (1867–1957), in the form of three papers published in 1909, 1911 and 1914.[5] Paish spoke with great authority. From 1900 to 1916, he was joint editor of the *Statist* – a financial weekly of a quality only just inferior to the *Economist*; he became sole editor thereafter. Paish was an authority on British and American railway statistics; he was the author of publications on railways, and a member of the Departmental Committee of the Board of Trade on Railway Accounts and Statistics from 1906 to

1908. During the early years of the First World War, Paish, assisted by J. M. Keynes from January 1915, served as Special Adviser on financial and economic matters to the Chancellor of the Exchequer, David Lloyd George. Others have followed him, but it is Paish's figures for foreign investment that matter and they are reproduced in simplified form as Table 1.1 below:

*Table* 1.1 Paish's estimate of Britain's portfolio investment abroad, 31 December 1913 (figures in £million, rounded to the nearest hundred thousand)

| | |
|---|---|
| Argentina | 319.6 |
| Australia | 332.1 |
| Brazil | 148.0 |
| Canada and Newfoundland | 514.9 |
| India and Ceylon | 378.8 |
| Mexico | 99.0 |
| New Zealand | 84.3 |
| Russia | 66.6 |
| South Africa | 370.2 |
| USA | 754.6 |
| The rest | 646.6 |
| Total | 3714.7 |

*Source*: Paish (1914). Paish allowed a further £300 million for 'direct' investment.

There has been no looking back. Paish supplied the base for the 'classics': the two Hobsons (J. A.[6] and C. K.[7]), Rudolf Hilferding,[8] and V. I. Lenin.[9] Herbert Feis, whose *Europe, the World's Banker, 1870–1914* (first published in 1930) is a recognised authority on British investment overseas for the critical decades before the First World War, used Paish for his basic numbers; his tables for long-term, publicly issued British capital investment in other lands and for the fields of employment of such capital were adapted with modifications from Paish's tables in the *Statist* Supplement of 14 February 1914.[10]

Subsequently, Paish's figures, or Paish's modified by Feis, are to be found behind nearly every stock figure for Britain's investments overseas (portfolio and direct) at the outbreak of the First World War: Eugene Staley,[11] Leland Jenks,[12] Sir Robert Kindersley,[13] Sir Arthur Salter,[14] Ragnar Nurkse,[15] A. R. Hall,[16] Brinley Thomas,[17]

William Woodruff,[18] John Dunning,[19] Philip Cottrell[20] . . . Even J. H. Lenfant, in an interesting doctoral thesis submitted in 1949 in the course of which he suggested very substantial reductions on Paish's estimates, came finally to the conventional conclusion, taken from Paish, that the total volume of Britain's foreign investments at the end of 1913, portfolio and direct, 'was probably nearly £4000 mn.'.[21] The Paish/Feis figure reappears wherever it is required to illustrate or reinforce a particular argument – in the works of Sir Alec Cairncross, for example, to indicate the distribution of British investment among countries and functions,[22] or in William Kennedy's for the calculation of rates of return.[23] It is no surprise to see Paish published in the general textbooks. I have no wish to build straw men, but if I were to take simply a sample of the best of current textbooks, Paish's number, taken as a stock figure for just before the Great War, finds its way into Eric Hobsbawm,[24] Alan Milward and S. B. Saul,[25] Donald McCloskey[26] and Peter Mathias.[27]

The standard figure, in fact, is Paish – a figure that appears automatically even today both in theses on capital exports[28] and in specialist monographs for which some such starting point is required.[29] For Avner Offer, as recently as 1983, Paish's papers to the Royal Statistical Society of 1909 and 1911 have 'remained the foundation of subsequent research'.[30] Paish's total resurfaces as the convenient stock figure for the first chapter – 'background information' – of *External Financing in Latin America*, published by the United Nations' Economic Commission for Latin America, next to some even more doubtful figures from J. Fred Rippy.[31]

Admittedly, the route to Paish can be tortuous and misleading. Official figures under impressive authority – Britain's Board of Trade, the League of Nations, the Royal Institute of International Affairs, the United Nations – gain legitimacy with age and repetition. Lloyd George's 'Financial Statement' to the House of Commons of 4 May 1915 – an important event in war finance – declared the stock of Britain's foreign and colonial securities to be £4 billion. This was 'enormous wealth' and gave great consolation to Britons and their allies; but the unascribed figure came from Paish, by now Special Adviser to the Chancellor of the Exchequer.[32] *The Board of Trade Journal* began its annual series of estimates from 1923 with the totals from Paish's papers of 1909 and 1911; these were taken to represent the capital value of the stock of British investments abroad, from which the *Board of Trade Journal* proceeded to determine the income and return on British overseas investment.[33] A popular source for Britain's stock of overseas investment has been *The Problem of International Investment*, published by the Royal Institute of International Affairs (Chatham House) in 1937; its numbers were drawn from Feis whose source was Paish.[34] A later report of the Economic Group of Chatham House's 'Reconstruction Committee', published during the Second World War, naturally followed the parent publication, so that its author found it possible to announce, unequivocally, that the volume of Britain's foreign assets just before the First World War was 'in round figures, about £4000 million, yielding some £200 million a year'[35] – the figures were Paish's. The estimates published by the United Nations in 1949 are often taken as authoritative,[36] yet the British estimates come either directly from Paish or from a League of Nations publication that itself depended on Paish![37]

The snag is that Paish had not intended to supply a stock figure; the idea that he had done so was simply a misunderstanding – a misunderstanding that has confused the issue ever since. Paish was normally quite specific. By the end of 1913, he said, the sum of capital supplied by Great Britain to other lands had been brought to the great total of £3 700 000 000 so that by the time some allowance was made for direct investment – capital invested privately – Paish's combined total reached no less than £4 billion.[38] But he did not always make his meaning perfectly clear, and those who have taken him to have put forward a stock figure have had reason to do so. While claiming in his 1911 paper to have calculated 'the approximate amount of visible capital which we have supplied to other lands in the aggregate', Paish then talked in the same paper about a 'net total of our investment in other lands', by which he meant in practice no more than an aggregate of his annual estimates.[39] His estimate, for example, of British holdings of US railway securities in 1907–8 (£600 million net) was simply the sum of his annual aggregates (gross). For Paish himself, his flow (aggregate) and stock figures later became utterly confused. When he advised Lloyd George in 1914–15 he was thinking of 'stock'. When he prepared a pamphlet for the League of Nations Society, near the end of the War, he meant the 'flow' of British investment – nearly £4 billion over the past century.[40] When he commented on Josiah Stamp's paper to the Royal Statistical Society in 1919 he was back to 'stock'; Britain's assets abroad just before the war, he said, were 'about £4000 million'.[41]

Subsequently, Paish's accumulated aggregates have been

interpreted in common usage as a standard stock figure for securities held on 31 December 1913. 'Before the war', said the Chairman of Barclays Bank, giving evidence in 1929 before the Macmillan Committee, 'we used to hold £3 500 000 000 or some such amount of foreign investments in this country' (i.e. Paish without the Paish figure for 'direct' investment).[42] This is what Herbert Feis, speaking for scholars, assumed when he published, from Paish's tables, a breakdown of fields of employment of British capital publicly invested abroad 'as of December 1913'.[43] It was what Ernest Ludlow Bogart thought when he spoke of the total amount of British overseas investment *at the end of the December 1913* as estimated by Paish at about £4 billion.[44]

It would be fair to argue, then, that whatever Paish himself originally intended his figure of £4 billion is now broadly accepted for the *stock* of British investment, portfolio and direct, on 31 December 1913. Paish's methods have been disputed on many occasions but his number has survived among contemporaries, immediate successors, and subsequent generations to the present day. During the discussion of Paish's first paper, given before the Royal Statistical Society on 15 June 1909, Cornelius Rosenraad explained that much of the money included in Paish's estimates was not British at all.[45] At Paish's second paper (1911), after vigorous discussion, even the Chairman (Sir Richard Biddulph Martin) admitted politely in his vote of thanks that Paish's figures 'came out at an amazing total, and were higher perhaps than those not fully acquainted with the subject would have guessed'.[46] J. M. Keynes, speaking briefly at the same discussion, was wholly dismissive. He pointed out that the proper title of Paish's paper should have been the 'estimated amount of capital subscribed in London', rather than 'estimated foreign investments'. Under Keynes' alternative title, he said, it was subject to two substantial omissions:

> On the one hand, the author made no pretence of including the amount invested otherwise than by subscription in London; on the other, he could not allow fully for the capital originally subscribed in London but which had found its way abroad subsequently; several speakers [at the discussion] had shown that both these errors were likely to be large.[47]

Keynes, like others, was assuming that Paish had produced a figure for the stock of British investment overseas, and the second of his arguments did not apply to the aggregate figure that Paish had in mind. More powerful, and at much greater length, was the material published by the German economist Paul Arndt in 1915.[48] Arndt could see what had gone wrong with the numbers. He too missed the point that Paish had intended to supply a figure for 'flows' rather than 'stock'. But his criticism of Paish's general approach was none the less devastating, and he was justified in assuming that nobody in future would accept it without serious doubt.

Subsequently, such contemporary criticism has been largely ignored, and for understandable reasons. The timing of Paish's papers, shortly before the Great War, meant that hostilities turned minds in different directions and the real issues were obscured. Arndt was a German writing in German in a German journal in 1915; it was unlikely that anything he said would have reached a British audience. Criticism of the Paish 'method' has continued, but it has focused on individual failings in the construction of his estimates, broken down by country or by industry, rather than on the distinction between what Paish intended to do and what he has been thought to have done. By modern criteria the 'method' is confusing and primitive, but it is worth examining because Paish was the first to attempt a major estimate of this kind, and because Paish's figures, acknowledged to be his or not as the case may be, have been so profoundly influential ever since. As I shall explain later, they are also the only realistic base from which we can proceed.

## PAISH'S METHODS (1909 PAPER)

The most valuable of the three Paish papers (1909, 1911 and 1914) is undoubtedly the first. The second and third made some allowance for the points raised by critics; but both, in practice, made use of the 1909 totals and added or projected, more or less successfully, from the original series. It was the 1909 'methodology' that determined the shape taken by the others.

Paish's 1909 paper, 'Great Britain's Capital Investment in Other Lands', began from the figures published in the annual returns of the Commissioners of Inland Revenue. Returns for the tax year 1906/7 showed £79.6 million as the income on foreign investment (of which only government, municipal and railway securities were identified). Paish's own researches on the same classes of securities raised this amount to £82.8 million, to which he added a further £58 million, calculated from the declared profits of 2172 public companies operating abroad that had raised capital privately in Britain, the income of which was not identified separately for tax. These company reports covered the operating year 1907 and in some cases the early months of 1908. Paish's conclusion was that the income received in Britain from portfolio investment overseas was nearly £140 million.

In the second part of his 1909 paper, Paish turned his attention to the quantity of capital invested abroad that could be expected to produce an annual income of nearly £140 million. He does not explain how he reached his figures (indeed, his paper is remarkably short of explanations) but his total came to £2.7 billion for British investment abroad, which, taken in conjunction with his estimated income of £140 million, brought an annual return of 5.2 per cent. Paish must have obtained his figures for government, provincial and municipal borrowing from one or other of the contemporary reference books, most probably the *Stock Exchange Official Intelligence* (which published details of all securities, public or private, dealt in or known on British stock exchanges). Furthermore, Paish examined the annual reports of his 2172 companies with overseas operations. These were taken, presumably, from the files of the *Statist*. Scrutiny of 'the reports of as many of the companies as it is possible for a private person to secure' was a large enterprise. But it was not entirely impracticable since the balance sheet in all company accounts (attached to the annual reports) showed totals for share capital issued in ordinary and preference shares, and for any debenture stock issued and outstanding.

It might be said that the Paish figure for the end of 1907, for all its peculiarities, was a kind of 'stock' figure, although Paish described it himself as an aggregate of all British investment over the last sixty years. It must have been difficult or even impossible to be precise since a reference book like the *Stock Exchange Official Intelligence*, although it normally gave the amounts outstanding at current prices, did not always do so, while company accounts reported stock and share capital issued but did not discuss where and to whom it had been issued, who had actually subscribed, and what had happened to the ownership of those securities thereafter. On the other hand, loans and debentures listed on company accounts, while they shared these faults, were cited more helpfully as amounts still in existence.

What Paish had done, then, was to add up foreign borrowing

(government, municipal and railway), after which he annexed the share capital and debenture stock (nominal value) of as many British companies operating abroad for which information could be obtained, whether in utilities, finance, mining, land or whatever. His figures, although mainly drawn from London, incorporated identifiable borrowing from any part of the United Kingdom. Since Paish was interested above all in assessing the accumulated quantity of 'Great Britain's capital investments in other lands' over sixty years, he felt no need to take into account subsequent repatriation of securities bought originally by British investors but sold again thereafter. Furthermore, until after the discussion that followed his first paper (1909), he made no real deduction in his figures to take account of foreign ownership of loans issued in London. His accumulated 'flow' estimates, for all three papers, contain no allowance for portions of loans retained in London to cover underwriting and issue charges. The effect of these is substantial, and I shall be returning to them in the next chapter.

Paish, in his 1909 paper, was pioneering in an immensely complicated area of debate. Even as a calculation of the accumulated monies put by Britons into foreign securities over the last half century or longer, it is just as well to recognise that Paish's methods contained many misunderstandings. Paish does not give the origin of his figures for bonds and stock. But if, as seems likely, he was using the *Stock Exchange Official Intelligence*, he would have found no complete *history* of the issues; government/municipal loans once repaid or reorganised were no longer cited in the list. Nor did he have the issue price with which to calculate a realistic total. Similarly, with company accounts the figures cited are for ordinary stock at nominal values (not at the real price of original sale). Paul Arndt, for one, was deeply suspicious. After wrestling with Paish's estimates for 1908, 1909 and 1910 (published in Paish, 1911), Arndt concluded that Paish's method in the 1911 paper was so uncritical that he (Arndt) had become even more sceptical about the global figures first published by Paish in 1909, and there was no way by which Paish's methods could be checked or verified. In Arndt's opinion, anyone who took the trouble to study Paish's methodology must feel tempted to strike some £500 million off the Paish estimate for 1907–8; these estimates, almost entirely unexplained, became visibly more fragmentary the more one looked at the omissions in the methodology of the papers of 1911 and 1914.[49] To use a modern analogy, they were like the thirteenth chime of the clock, improbable in itself and casting doubt on all that had gone before. And it is true that F. W. Hirst, editor of the *Economist* at a time when it was producing figures on very much the same lines as Paish's *Statist*, four years after Paish and including the intervening years, arrived at an estimate of British investment abroad that, at £2.3 billion, removed £400 million – much like Arndt – from Paish's first figure (for 1907–8).[50]

## PAISH'S METHODS (1911 AND 1914 PAPERS)

The material gathered for Paish's 1911 and 1914 papers is much less complex and comprehensive. Paish simply kept an eye on capital issues on the London Stock Exchange, added them up (at the price of issue), made some minor deductions for unspecified items like foreign ownership of a portion of issues (although his numbers do not seem to indicate reductions on the scale he proclaimed), and applied a standard formula to his tabulated figures, namely 'calculated at the prices of issue [from 1911, at nominal prices], and excluding all conversion loans and shares issued to vendors'. The first occasion on which Paish broke down British portfolio investment by country was in his paper for 1911, and he made it quite clear that what he was again talking about was the total of British investment in each country over the years, not the stock of securities still held:

> The aggregate amount of capital which the Mother Country has provided for the British Dominions beyond the Seas is the great sum of £1 554 000 000. The aggregate of our investments in foreign countries is £1 638 000 000, of which 42 per cent is in the United States.

The two categories (Empire and foreign) add up to £3 192 000 000 for aggregated portfolio investment of Britons abroad up to the end of 1910.

Paish's paper of February 1914 took the figures to the end of 1913. He called his totals 'amounts subscribed' at the price of issue, which implied an unrealistic degree of accuracy: his figures (like the *Economist*'s) are for amounts issued rather than actually subscribed. They could not be otherwise, since they coincide almost exactly with the *Economist*'s totals of issues described simply as 'offered' for subscription in 1909 and 1913. In effect, Paish's 'subscriptions' were also 'offers'; the omissions and sophistications described by him during the discussion of his 1911 paper must presumably account for such differences between the two series as remain. As he put it himself, he was citing £250 million 'publicly issued securities' for Canada over the last seven years (1907–13 inclusive) and £118 million of new capital for Argentina, summed up from the table on the previous page of his paper. After adding the issues on London for 1911–13 to the £3.2 billion of 31 December 1910, Paish arrived at an aggregate total for Britain's portfolio investment overseas, by the end of 1913, of £3.7 billion.

Paish's 'method', for his second and third papers, was simply the addition of *London* issues to his global total for 1907–8. It is perfectly understandable that Paish should have acted as he did, although perhaps less so that his full figure for 31 December 1913 should have been accepted so uncritically ever since. Paish was a busy man, and he had no time to return to the compilation of figures on the scale of his first paper (1909) for 1907–8. None the less, what he had done was to patch together two quite different estimates. His total for 31 December 1913, which added 30 per cent to his figure for the end of 1907, was quite clearly an aggregate of London issues ('flows') over six further years, stapled on to a very different variety of 'stock' estimate, far more comprehensive, for the end of 1907.

## PAISH'S SUCCESSORS AND THE 'DIRECT' METHOD

This was all very random and arbitrary. W. R. Lawson, commenting on the best of the Paish papers (the first), described Paish's research as 'an heroic effort to solve an insoluble problem'; he added that for all the labour and ability that Paish had bestowed, Paish himself would be the first to acknowledge for his calculations that 'there was not a table among them which could be accepted as scientific statistics'.[51]

The burden of the discussion on Paish's 1911 paper was that much more analysis was required. This was true. But Paish had made a start, and the 'direct' method – the laborious tabulation of portfolio issues, in association with more or less informed guesses for investment that did not pass through the Stock Exchange – is still the best (and perhaps the only) means by which we can arrive either at an aggregate of British portfolio investment overseas over half a century, or at an approximate stock figure for British ownership just before the First World War. My own preoccupation is with 'stock', the actual, outstanding amount of foreign investment held by Britons resident in the UK just before the war, and I shall explain my revision of Paish's total below. Others have made great progress with 'flows' for the half century or longer before 1914.

The confusion between the two is not confined to Paish. Jacob Viner's calculations for Canada, to which, in Lenfant's opinion, 'there is little that could be added in the way of comprehensiveness or accuracy', seem to have suffered in much the same way. Viner, like Paish, calculated something like a stock figure for the total of British investment in Canada for 1899, to which he added a gross increase, annual amounts or 'flows', for the peak period of British investment in Canada, to make a total for 1913. Viner's estimates are not so vulnerable as Paish's, since Canada was so large a borrower and so openly dependent on London investors. All the same, like Paish, Viner has been supposed to have calculated a stock figure for British investment in Canada when his figures in fact reflect a form of stock in 1899, followed by undisguised flows for the important period of foreign investment in Canada, 1899 to 1913. Firestone, a respected authority on the economic history of Canada, took Viner's figure (via Frank A. Knox[52]) as a stock estimate.[53] In an impressive volume on the historical statistics of Canada, Viner's figure for British non-resident investment in Canada appears again as a stock figure for 1913, followed by the Knox estimate for 1914 that supposedly confirms the scale (although, since it came itself from Viner, it does no such thing).[54] It is a familiar story . . .

Paish was writing some seventy-five years ago. We shall be coming to the alternative balance of payments method by which the volume of overseas investment is now more commonly, if unreliably, measured. But first it must be said that Paish's 'direct' method has been improved and extended by many. Herbert Feis followed Paish's figures for the end of 1913, with the exception of increases for Australasia, Russia and Turkey.[55] Feis himself was writing a general history of foreign investment, and he did not pretend to arrive at his own set of estimates; he had no 'methodology' of his own.

It was Sir Robert Kindersley, in a series of annual articles published in the *Economic Journal* for the decade leading up to the Second World War, who made the most professional use of direct estimates. Like Paish, Kindersley confined himself to government and municipal securities listed in the *Stock Exchange Official Intelligence*, the service of which was in any degree effected in London. Again like Paish (but more so), Kindersley included some

3000 British companies whose securities were officially marketable in London but which operated abroad, in addition to which he steadily gained access to up to seventy banks and issuing houses for which, as chairman of Lazards, he had a special lien. Unlike Paish, Kindersley made allowance for some categories of shipping (£12 million in 1929 and £15.2 million in 1930), and he added a sizeable amount for private investment through foreign exchanges or in private companies and ventures whose seat of operation was abroad.

Kindersley, whose focus was on the return to be had on investment abroad, needed a stock figure. Unlike Paish, he became particularly interested in the problem of repayments. His figures for 'stock' were the first useful estimates of their kind. Kindersley set out to establish (a) the total nominal amount of British capital overseas outstanding at the end of each year, (b) the income derived therefrom, (c) the volume of annual repayments, and (d) the 'new money' saved each year for further investment abroad (that is, the British subscription to new issues, less the sum repaid during the year). However, Kindersley's total did not include what he described as 'the considerable amount of investment in property, mortgages, etc., and in securities not regularly dealt in on the London market', of which US dollar bonds and shares formed a large amount. In each subsequent year Kindersley improved his method and coverage; his last article, for 1938, was a substantial refinement on the first for 1928.[56]

Kindersley's 'direct' estimates, of course, were for the inter-war years, long after Paish. They are interesting for his greater refinement in the use of the direct method, and for the scale they established in relation to Paish's estimates before 1914. A. R. Hall's direct estimates, like Paish's, are for 'flows', as are the complementary estimates by J. D. Bailey.[57] J. Fred Rippy has produced a stock estimate for British investment in Latin America for December 1913 which he took from figures published by the *South American Journal*;[58] they are an improvement on the Chatham House survey of 1937,[59] but they suffered from the 'Paishian' faults of being confined to issues on the London Stock Exchange, of making no allowance for foreign borrowing in London, and of including no provision for such phenomena as repayments or amortisations. H. S. Ferns, who had the unhappy experience of being 'supervised' by Rippy at Chicago, described him as being 'a prolific but uncritical and undescriminating scholar . . . fascinated and impressed by numbers; it did not matter what they were or whence they came'.[60]

Until recently Matthew Simon's estimates have supplied the most up-to-date direct estimates of 'flows'. Simon, basing his figures on a very comprehensive study of monthly calls on the London Stock Exchange (extracted from the *Investor's Monthly Manual*), produced an aggregate figure for new British portfolio investment overseas that amounted to £3.9 billion by the end of 1913. Since he was identifying annual flows he did not need to allow either for repatriation or for foreign ownership.[61] Unfortunately, Simon died before he had been able to refine the distribution of investment beyond Canada,[62] and the heir to his 'data-bank', Irving Stone, has not been successful as yet in making much sense of the material that still remains in New York.[63] Some of the Simon data, however, has been used by Michael Edelstein,[64] and the most recent enterprise of its kind, the recalculation of 'flows' by Lance Davis and Robert Huttenback, is now in the press. Davis and Huttenback were able to employ much the same sources on new issues as Simon, and they have been examining the spatial and industrial distribution that Simon had never had the time to undertake himself. But like Simon they have not tried to derive a figure for British as compared with foreign investors, nor are they concerned with the calculation of a stock estimate for Britain's overseas investment at any single date.[65]

## THE 'INDIRECT' (BALANCE OF PAYMENTS) METHOD

The other approach to the estimation of investment overseas is the 'indirect' method associated, from the 1950s, most particularly with Albert Imlah. Both direct and indirect methods have been understood and practised since before the First World War. J. M. Keynes had both in mind when he distinguished between the direct method (as meaning the derivation of a figure from the available statistics for capital investments, supplemented where necessary by doubtful estimates), and the indirect approach that took evidence from the balance of trade. C. K. Hobson used both in his classic *Export of Capital* (1914). Lenfant's thesis (1949) drew separately on both. Most recently, Michael Edelstein has used figures both from Imlah and Paish. Textbooks use both indiscriminately . . .[66]

By what can only be described as an accident, the 'flow' (aggregated) figure from Paish, estimated by the direct method, and the 'stock' total calculated from the overall balance on current account, indirectly estimated, come within reach of each other.

Although they measure very different things, the conjunction is impressive enough to have convinced many of the rightness of both. Imlah's own conclusion, no doubt a cause of much satisfaction at the time, was that:

> the very close correspondence with the more studied and credible estimates [Giffen, Paish, Hobson and Jenks] of the value of British foreign investment at so many points along the way invites a measure of confidence in the validity of [Imlah's] series on British credits accumulated abroad.[67]

And many have found comfort in that similarity ever since.

As I have said, Imlah was not the first to calculate what Noel Butlin defines as 'the residual between current account credits and debits',[68] but it is Imlah's work in the 1950s that underpins all that follows – Mitchell, Deane and Cole, Dunning, Feinstein and Matthews.[69] Imlah constructed his estimates for income from abroad from Paish. Feinstein's figures are 'adjusted Imlah'. Matthews followed Feinstein. The chain was complete. Imlah is to 'indirect' estimates what Paish is to 'direct' estimates; Imlah's estimates – among those who have appreciated the 'method' – are 'generally accepted as the best available [for] Britain's net lending abroad'.[70]

If Imlah had genuinely been able to produce, by his method, so convincing and authoritative a figure for the stock of British investment overseas, no more needs to be said. It was a bold attempt, and the 'method' must be taken seriously if only to show why, in the end and with every possible reservation, we are forced to start any realistic revision from the direct method and from Paish.

The argument depends, as much as anything else, on what questions are asked, and what answers are expected.[71] The 'direct' method tells us nothing about the resale of securities – what is known as the secondary market. It does not attempt to identify short-term credits. If it is intended to supply a 'flow' figure, it makes no allowance for commissions and expenses deducted from an issue before it reaches its destination. Investment in shipping, although relevant in part to a balance of payments figure, is not appropriate for a direct estimate, and is disallowed as such by Leland Jenks.[72] Above all, the direct method has not been able to furnish a convincing figure for foreign ownership of securities bought on British markets, for amortisation and repatriation.

The 'indirect' method, on the other hand, cannot supply an

amount for the capital floated in London on a particular date; it does not indicate to which country it went, in what volume and for what purpose; it cannot show who bought the issues, at what rate and when. Oscar Morgenstern found that for his own purpose (the study of international financial transactions and business cycles) the balance of payments approach was unhelpful.[73] Robert Kindersley pointed to the problems in remittances/non-remittances registered in Board of Trade returns, and added that he could find no direct relation between the income he himself was describing (interest and dividends accruing to UK investors) and 'income from oversea investments as understood in a discussion of the United Kingdom balance of payments' for which net profits were the important consideration.[74] Mira Wilkins repeats that 'residual' estimates do not separate short-term from long-term, do not identify portfolio investment, do not measure gross movements (only net), and do not thereby distinguish between foreign and domestic inflows and outflows.[75] Sidney Pollard is surely right to complain that while each of the methods, 'direct' and 'balance of payments', seem to come to a similar conclusion, they ought *not* to have done so:

> it may, of course, be that by some miracle all these divergencies cancel out, but the suspicion must remain that there has been a certain amount of fudging to achieve the recorded overall agreement, especially since the volumes for the intermediate years differ widely.[76]

The point is serious, and it strikes deep into the heart of the profession. Imlah's balance of payments estimates have been described as 'theoretically and conceptually sound'. Given the existence of accurate data, this may even be the case. But Peter Clarke, when quoting Sir Alexander Cairncross's 'salutary caution' against the 'simple trust' we have given to figures for even the period after the Second World War, has reminded us of 'those economic historians who have regarded quantitative data as possessing a privileged degree of certainty'.[77] And indeed the figures quoted by Imlah, and those derived from them, may be unworkable.

Imlah's calculations and tables for Britain's balance of payments over the century before 1914 are an improvement on Hobson and even on Cairncross. His methods were described first in his article of 1952 and later in his book *Economic Elements in the Pax Britannica* (1958). Imlah explained that in calculating the accumulating balance of credit and thus the effective export of British capital for the century 1816–1913, he had taken into account the balance of visible trade (merchandise, gold and silver bullion and specie, ship sales, business services, insurance, brokerage, shipping commissions, and net earnings of shipping), the balance of further current items (emigrant funds, tourist expenditures, smuggling and other unrecorded items), and the balance of interest and dividends. From these he had made up a total annual figure for the whole period (1816–1913) for 'net income available from investment abroad', or, to put it another way, the balances earned on current account each year.

Imlah had gone far beyond the pioneers. The difficulty in the 1952 article, which became even more evident in the larger amount of space available in his book of 1958, was that the figures were simply not up to it – his methods were impracticable on existing data. A century of figures meant in practice much projection backwards and forwards from whatever 'reliable' figure might be identified. This had curious and unconvincing results, and I propose to take four of the more important of the series employed by Imlah to illustrate my point:

1. *Balance on business services*: insurance, brokerage, shipping commissions, etc. These were taken from Robert Giffen's estimated earnings in this category at 2½ per cent on the total value of British foreign trade, including bullion, for the period 1854–80. Imlah then added some unsubstantiated ups and downs of Giffen's rate to cover the entire period back to 1816 and up to 1913.
2. *Balance on business services: profit on goods and services.* Imlah's base figures were drawn from Leland Jenks, who himself had taken them from Stephen Bourne, an unreliable source.[78] Jenks allowed a flat 5 per cent on the total value of imports and of British-produced exports to represent the profit on foreign trade for 1854 to 1880. Imlah then projected this rate forwards and backwards, raising and lowering it from time to time on what seem to be very slender and subjective grounds.
3. *Balance on business services*: net credits from shipping. This was an important series, not exceeded by the income from foreign investments until the 1870s. Imlah took these also from Giffen, but in this case from a single figure – Giffen's estimates of average earnings per net ton of sail (£5) and steam (£15) for

1880, much criticised even when first discussed by Giffen in 1882.[79] The 1880 figure, with some corrections, lay behind Imlah's whole series for the century 1816–1913.[80]

4. *Balance on interest and dividends from foreign investments*. For present purposes, this column in the Imlah series is the most important; the total for the whole period was calculated at £4.7 billion. If this set of figures is right, as W. P. Kennedy says, 'then the series that results, net foreign investment, should be roughly correct'.[81] Imlah followed the method first established by C. K. Hobson in 1914. Hobson took the ratio between the £84 million identified by the Inland Revenue as the income on certain classes of overseas investment for the tax year 1906 to 1907, against Paish's estimate of a further, unidentified income for 1907 of £60 million (that is, a ratio of 84:60). Imlah made some crude adjustments so that the tax year 1906 to 1907 could be employed in association with the calendar year 1907. He set a more realistic limit than Hobson to the value of the Revenue figures, starting only from the Coupon Act of 1885. But he then proceeded, like Hobson, to project this single ratio back to 1885 and forward (from 1907) to 1913. When Hobson first published his 'method', a contemporary critic at once made the point that any assumption that such a ratio remained constant for forty years was supported by no real evidence.[82] To Paul Arndt, Hobson's belief that the ratio was the same in 1907 as it had been for the whole period between 1875 and 1912 was not only very arbitrary but most unlikely to be correct; Hobson's estimates for income from abroad (and hence, by derivation, Imlah's) were 'wertlos'.[83] Imlah's method *before* 1886 was to apply unexplained percentages to his estimates for annually accumulated balances: 6.6 per cent in the early years after 1815, 3.5 per cent for the early 1830s, 6 per cent by 1835–6, 4 per cent for 1841–2, 'and so on through successive booms and depressions' – guessed percentages on guessed totals.

The total for all four of Imlah's columns, 1816 to 1913, reaches the gigantic sum of £11.5 billion, and the potential for error is therefore immense.

## CONCLUSION

For all its imperfections, there is no practical alternative as yet to the 'direct' method, and the 'direct' method effectively means George Paish. Imlah and the 'indirect' method have had disciples at the highest level of professional competence, and no doubt will continue to find support; some day, somewhere, it may be possible to assemble sufficiently satisfactory data from which the 'indirect' method may be rehabilitated. That day has yet to come. Meanwhile, if we are to construct what remains the object of this book – a stock figure for British investment abroad on the eve of the First World War – we must return to the 'direct' method and, at least as a starting point, to Sir George Paish.

## Notes

1. Felix Schuster, 'Foreign Trade and the Money Market', *Journal of the Institute of Bankers*, XXV, 2 (Feb. 1904) p. 120.
2. D. C. M. Platt, *Foreign Finance in Continental Europe and the USA, 1815–1870: Quantities, Origins, Functions and Distribution* (1984).
3. A. T. K. Grant, *A Study of the Capital Market in Britain from 1919–1936* (2nd edn 1967) p. 120.
4. Minutes of Evidence, *Report of the Committee on Finance and Industry*, vol. 1 (HMSO, 1931) Q. 4279.
5. Paish (1909), Paish (1911) and Paish (1914).
6. J. A. Hobson, *An Economic Interpretation of Investment* (1911) p. 61, although Hobson, who drew heavily on Paish (1911), realised that Paish was talking about an aggregate.
7. C. K. Hobson, *The Export of Capital* (1914) pp. 162, 202, 204.
8. Rudolf Hilferding, *Finance Capital: A Study of the Latest Phase of Capitalist Development* (trans. 1981; 1st edn 1910) p. 428, fn. 9.
9. V. I. Lenin, 'Imperialism, the Highest Stage of Capitalism', in *Selected Works* (Moscow, 1930) vol. 1, pt. 2, p. 496 (and many other editions).
10. (New York, 1965 edn) pp. 23, 27.
11. Eugene Staley, *War and the Private Investor: A Study in the Relations of International Politics and International Private Investment* (Chicago, 1935) p. 525.
12. L. H. Jenks, 'British Experience with Foreign Investments', *Journal of Economic History*, IV (1944) p. 68.
13. Sir Robert Kindersley, annual series on capital exports, *Economic Journal* (1930–9) passim.
14. Sir Arthur Salter, *Foreign Investment* (Princeton, 1951) pp. 4–5. Salter's figures came from the Royal Institute of International Affairs; these, in turn, were from Feis, who drew on Paish . . .
15. Ragnar Nurkse, 'International Investment Today in the Light of

Nineteenth Century Experience', *Economic Journal* (Dec. 1954) p. 750, fn. 1.

16. A. R. Hall, *The London Capital Market and Australia, 1870–1914* (Canberra, 1963) p. 11.
17. Brinley Thomas, 'The Historical Record of International Capital Movements to 1913', in J. H. Adler (ed.) *Capital Movements and Economic Development* (New York, 1967) pp. 6–7.
18. William Woodruff, *Impact of Western Man: A Study of Europe's Role in the World Economy, 1750–1960* (New York, 1966) p. 150. Woodruff's figures for 1914 are generally based on Eugene Staley, and Staley's figures (fn. 11 above) come from Paish.
19. John H. Dunning, *Studies in International Investment* (1970) p. 17, quoting the United Nations, itself based on Paish.
20. P. L. Cottrell, *British Overseas Investment in the Nineteenth Century* (1975) p. 11.
21. J. H. Lenfant, 'British Capital Exports, 1900–1913' (unpublished Ph.D. thesis, University of London, 1949) pp. 68, 70, fn. 12.
22. Sir Alexander Cairncross, *Home and Foreign Investment 1870–1913* (Cambridge, 1953) p. 184. A more regionally based scholar does the same: S. Herbert Frankel, *Capital Investment in Africa: Its Cause and Effects* (1938) pp. 149–50.
23. W. P. Kennedy, 'Foreign Investment, Trade and Growth in the United Kingdom, 1870–1913', *Explorations in Economic History*, XI, 1 (1974) p. 432.
24. E. J. Hobsbawm, *Pelican Economic Hisotry of Britain, Vol. 3: From 1750 to the Present Day, Industry and Empire* (1969) p. 152.
25. Alan S. Milward and S. B. Saul, *The Development of the Economies of Continental Europe, 1850–1914* (1977) p. 493.
26. Donald N. McCloskey, *Enterprise and Trade in Victorian Britain, Essays in Historical Economics* (1981) p. 149.
27. Peter Mathias, *The First Industrial Nation: An Economic History of Britain, 1700–1914* (2nd edn 1983) p. 298.
28. For example, John Michael Atkins, 'British Overseas Investment, 1918–1931' (Ph.D. thesis, University of London, 1968) p. 1.
29. For example, Geoffrey Jones, *The State and the Emergence of the British Oil Industry* (1981) pp. 47–8; Peter Buckley and Brian R. Roberts, *European Direct Investment in the USA before World War I* (1982) p. 14, where the sources include Staley, Dunning and Cleona Lewis, all of whom have drawn on Paish.
30. A. Offer, 'Empire and Social Reform: British Overseas Investment and Domestic Politics', *Historical Journal*, 26, 1 (1983) p. 125.
31. United Nations publication sales no. 65. II.G.4, p. 9, and J. Fred Rippy, *British Investments in Latin America, 1822–1949* (Minneapolis, 1959).
32. 71 *House of Commons Debates* 5s.1010. Paish was clearly responsible for a Treasury paper of late 1914 which had advised the Chancellor that Britain had assets of £4 billion currently invested abroad: paper quoted by Avner Offer, 'Empire and Social Reform', p. 129, fn. 51.
33. *Board of Trade Journal*, 29 March 1923, pp. 384–5.

34. The practice was infectious, and similar figures lie behind the report of the United Nations' Department of Economic and Social Affairs in its publication on 'The Growth of Foreign Investments in Latin America', where 'the total (nominal) value of foreign investments in Latin America in 1914 may be put at about $8.5 billion, or almost one fifth of world-wide long-term foreign investments', $3.7 billion of which are supposed to have come from the United Kingdom: quoted in Marvin D. Bernstein (ed.), *Foreign Investment in Latin America* (New York, 1966) p. 36. The $3.7 billion figure (unacknowledged) is almost exactly the figure in Paish (1914).
35. H. W. Arndt, *The Economic Lessons of the Nineteen Thirties* (1944) p. 110.
36. United Nations, *International Capital Movements during the Inter-War Period* (New York, 1949) p. 3, fn. 3.
37. League of Nations, *The Course and Phases of the World Economic Depression* (Geneva, 1931) p. 28. The League did not give its sources, but it was quite obviously drawing on Paish.
38. Paish (1914), p. v.
39. Paish (1911), pp. 167, 187.
40. Paish, *The Economic Interdependence of Nations* (1918) p. 17.
41. J. C. Stamp, 'The Wealth and Income of the Chief Powers', *Journal of the Royal Statistical Society*, 82 (1919), discussion p. 497.
42. Mr Frederick Craufurd Goodenough, 13 December 1929: minutes of evidence, *Report of the Committee on Finance and Industry*, vol. I, Q. 640.
43. H. Feis, *Europe: The World's Banker*, p. 27.
44. E. L. Bogart, *War Costs and their Financing* (New York, 1921) p. 14.
45. Paish (1909), discussion pp. 484–5.
46. Paish (1911), discussion p. 188.
47. Ibid., p. 195.
48. Paul Arndt, 'Neue Beiträge zur Frage der Kapitalanlage im Ausland', *Zeitschrift für Socialwissenschaft*, N.F., VI (1915) article no. 3 ('Zur Statistik der Kapitalanlagen im Ausland'). I am most grateful to Professor Sidney Pollard (University of Bielefeld) for sending me a copy of this important article.
49. Ibid., pp. 311, 301.
50. F. W. Hirst in Porter, *Progress of the Nation*, p. 701.
51. Paish (1909), p. 493.
52. Frank A. Knox's 'excursus' on the Canadian balance of payments in Herbert Marshall *et al.*, *Canadian–American Industry: A Study of International Investment* (New Haven, Conn., 1938) pp. 296–325.
53. Jacob Viner, *Canada's Balance of International Indebtedness, 1900–1913* (Cambridge, Mass., 1924).
54. M. C. Urquhart and K. A. H. Buckley (eds), *Historical Statistics of Canada* (Toronto, 1965) series F 193–207, p. 169.
55. Feis, *Europe: The World's Banker*, pp. 23ff.
56. Kindersley's papers started from 'British Foreign Investments in 1928', *Economic Journal*, XV (June 1930) and continued annually until 'British

Oversea Investments, 1938', in the *Economic Journal* (December 1939), and see fn. 13 above.

57. Hall has contributed much in this area, starting from *The London Capital Market and Australia, 1870–1914* (Canberra, 1963) based on an earlier, London Ph.D. thesis. J. D. Bailey's unpublished Oxford D. Phil. thesis of 1957, 'Australian Company Borrowing (1870–93)', uses the direct method, while Butlin, *Australia's Domestic Product, Investment and Foreign Borrowing*, uses both.
58. Rippy, *British Investments in Latin America.*
59. Royal Institute of International Affairs, *The Republics of South America* (Oxford, 1937) p. 182.
60. H. S. Ferns, *Reading from Left to Right: One Man's Political History* (Toronto, 1983) p. 275.
61. Matthew Simon, 'The Pattern of New British Portfolio Foreign Investment, 1865–1914', in J. H. Adler (ed.), *Capital Markets and Economic Development* (New York, 1967) p. 40, fn. 1. Another version is his 'The Enterprise and Industrial Composition of New British Portfolio Foreign Investment, 1865–1914', *Journal of Development Studies*, 3, 3 (April, 1967) pp. 280–92, and he published an article with Segal in the *Journal of Economic History* of 1961, the improved version of which is published in Adler, *Capital Markets*.
62. Matthew Simon, 'New British Investment in Canada, 1865–1914', *Canadian Journal of Economics*, III, 2 (May 1970).
63. I. Stone, 'British Direct and Portfolio Investment in Latin America before 1914', *Journal of Economic History*, XXXVII, 3 (Sept. 1977) pp. 690–1.
64. Michael Edelstein has published a great deal. The most useful for this theme are his two articles 'The Determinants of UK Investment Abroad, 1870–1913: The US Case', *Journal of Economic History*, XXXIV, 4 (December 1974), and 'Realized Rates of Return on UK Home and Overseas Investment in the Age of High Imperialism', *Explorations in Economic History*, 13 (1976), and his recent book, *Overseas Investment in the Age of High Imperialism: The United Kingdom, 1850–1914* (1982).
65. Lance Davis and Robert A. Huttenback, 'The Export of Finance: 1865–1914' (chapter in a forthcoming book). A first version has been published under the same title in the *Journal of Imperial and Commonwealth History*, XIII, 3 (May 1985) pp. 28–76.
66. For example, Derek H. Aldcroft and Harry W. Richardson, *The British Economy, 1870–1939* (1969) pp. 64, 84–7, and Philip S. Bagwell and G. E. Mingay, *Britain and America, 1850–1939: A Study of Economic Change* (1970) pp. 106, 108, 111.
67. Albert Imlah, 'British Balance of Payments and Export of Capital, 1816–1913', *Economic History Review*, 2nd ser. V, 2 (1952) p. 208, where he mentions the fact that the balances that he constructed could be 'checked at certain points with the more credible results achieved by other investigators who have made different approaches to the problem' (i.e. Paish and users of the direct method). Also his *Economic Elements*

*in the Pax Britannica: Studies in British Foreign Trade in the Nineteenth Century* (Cambridge, Mass., 1958) p. 80.

68. N. Butlin, *Australian Domestic Product, Investment and Foreign Borrowing*, p. 405.
69. So far as they touch the quantity of foreign investment: B. R. Mitchell, *Abstract of British Historical Statistics* (Cambridge, 1962) pp. 333–4; Phyllis Deane and W. A. Cole, *British Economic Growth 1688–1959: Trends and Structure* (Cambridge, 1967 edn) pp. 36, 166–7, 175, 266, 274, 308, 332; Tom Huston and John H. Dunning, *UK Industry Abroad* (London, 1976) p. 62; Feinstein, *National Income, Expenditure and Output*, p. 205; R. C. O. Matthews, C. H. Feinstein and J. C. Odling-Smee, *British Economic Growth, 1856–1973* (Oxford, 1980) p. v.
70. C. H. Feinstein, *National Income, Expenditure and Output*, p. 28. Edelstein likewise describes Imlah's estimates as the 'most authoritative' of their kind: *Overseas Investment in the Age of High Imperialism*, p. 18.
71. Perhaps the most lucid explanation of the two contrasting methods, direct and indirect, is to be found in Butlin, *Australian Domestic Product, Investment and Foreign Borrowing*, pp. 405–7.
72. L. Jenks, *Export of Capital*, p. 341.
73. O. Morgenstern, *International Financial Transactions and Business Cycles* (Princeton, N.J., 1959) p. 556.
74. Kindersley, 'British Overseas Investments in 1931', *Economic Journal* (June 1933) pp. 202–3.
75. M. Wilkins, letter to author, 26 February 1985.
76. S. Pollard, 'Capital Exports 1870–1914 – Harmful or Beneficial?', slightly reworded in the published version: *Economic History Review*, 2s. XXXVIII, 4 (1985) p. 492–3.
77. P. Clarke, 'Guessing at the Future', *Times Literary Supplement*, 21 June 1985, p. 683.
78. S. Bourne, *Trade, Population and Food: A Series of Papers on Economics and Statistics* (London, 1880), and his previous article in the *Journal of the Statistical Society* (March 1877).
79. Robert Giffen, 'The Use of Import and Export Statistics', *Journal of the Statistical Society* (June 1882) pp. 181–296, and Giffen's paper 'The Excess of Imports', *Journal of the Royal Statistical Society* (March 1899) pp. 1–82.
80. The real difficulty (in the case of Imlah and others) of computing realistic proportions for investment in shipping is reviewed exhaustively in Douglas North and Alan Heston, 'The Estimation of Shipping Earnings in Historical Studies of the Balance of Payments', *Canadian Journal of Economics and Political Science*, 26, 2 (1960) pp. 265–76. As for a stock figure, Robert Kindersley does in fact take shipping companies into account within his Group 2 (British companies operating abroad). His estimates are for the inter-war period, of course, when the numbers were much different, but within his own limited definition they are not likely to have been large, even before (the share capital for 1929 was calculated at just under £12 million and it was £15.2 million for 1930). Kindersley explained that he took into account only those

companies the trading of which was almost entirely between ports in foreign waters; much of the earnings on British capital placed in the shipping trade between the UK and the rest of the world was derived from abroad, but since no part of the capital employed by these companies was actually spent abroad their services might conveniently be regarded as an export: 'consequently it is preferable not to regard this capital as a foreign investment': Kindersley, 'British Foreign Investments in 1930', *Economic Journal*, 42 (June 1932) p. 182. Certainly, Leland Jenks excluded shipping for his direct estimates in *Export of Capital* (p. 341). Yet J. A. Hobson added £200–300 million for capital invested in shipping: *An Economic Interpretation of Investment* (n.d., ?1911) pp. 61–2.

81. W. P. Kennedy, 'Foreign Investment, Trade and Growth', p. 441.
82. J.C.S., review of Hobson's *Export of Capital* in the *Journal of the Royal Statistical Society* (Jan. 1915) p. 96.
83. P. Arndt, 'Neue Beiträge', pp. 305ff.

# Part II
# The Direct Method Reassessed

# 2 The Stock of British Investment Overseas on the Eve of the First World War: A Revised Estimate

In Part I, I argued that the only feasible route to a stock figure for British investment overseas just before the First World War was 'direct' – the compilation of numbers for securities bought and sold on a stock exchange. The 'balance of payments method', whatever its theoretical advantages, has not yet reached a point when it can realistically be expected to supply any such thing, besides which its practitioners have themselves aimed at a different kind of result.

As I have said earlier, the 'direct' method started from Sir George Paish. Since Paish thought himself to be dealing not with a stock figure for 31 December 1913 but with aggregates over half a century – and became somewhat confused in the process – there were instances within his figures both of overestimation and of underestimation, of double counts and of elements important to 'flow' figures but not to 'stock'. This chapter attempts to suggest a 'stock' figure that starts from Paish, yet takes his omissions into account.

## NON-BRITISH PURCHASES ON THE LONDON STOCK EXCHANGE

The weakness that lies at the heart of all Paish figures (the focus of much criticism from the beginning) is the omission, until the end of 1907, of any allowance in his 'British' figures for foreign ownership of securities bought through the London Stock Exchange. Paish acknowledged this in the discussion that followed his first paper to the Royal Statistical Society in 1909, and he claimed to have included an allowance of 10 per cent from 1908 to the end of 1913.

The point is important, both for the estimation of 'flows' and for 'stock'. London's market for securities, more particularly before the First World War, was genuinely international. In 1907, the key year for Paish's first estimate, London was 'still the greatest of all European money markets . . . when London becomes active the Continent invests and speculates here upon a considerable scale'.[1] Many large foreign firms had offices or branches in the City intended specifically 'to buy and sell on account of foreign bourses' – indeed, the existence of so much foreign business in London was the reason why the London Stock Exchange was closed on 31 July 1914, only three days after the Austrian declaration of war on Serbia, when resident foreign firms found it impossible to collect what was due to them from abroad.[2]

Overseas banks and agencies (foreign and Empire) are said to have handled as much as 20 per cent of London's investment abroad in the decade before the war. The *Economist* found that for London, as the money market of the world, 'new applications' for public subscription offered 'a fair index of the requirements of the world',[3] even if Britons were not themselves the source. A loan advertised in London and recommended to clients abroad could attract foreign subscriptions either through foreign agencies in London or direct. Great Britain acted simply as the principal intermediary between Europe and other parts of the world for the placing abroad of foreign securities issued in London; it was 'an honest broker taking over – to a great extent with the money of his customers – the loans of other nations'.[4]

The reasons were obvious. London was cheaper and more convenient than Paris or Berlin, and New York was as yet almost entirely a market for domestic securities. The convertibility of the pound sterling, and Britain's worldwide network of shipping, trade and finance, combined to make London a 'home for funds irrespective of interest rates'.[5] French investors, in the latter part of the 1900s, developed a strong interest in US 'rails': 'France is not in as close or intimate connection with the US as England, and the French market therefore looks to a certain extent to the London market for information and guidance.'[6] French investors in Russian bonds may actually have preferred to deal in London rather than in Paris, and prices in London, after heavy French buying, rose above Paris.[7]

London was a safe destination for refugee capital in difficult times. It was professionally organised and well informed. It provided, for the foreign investor, 'a potent source of tax evasion',[8] and the tendency of the French Income Tax Bill was reportedly (1907) to increase French purchases on the London Stock Exchange and to diminish investment at home; 'already this week there has been good buying [in London] on French account of South American securities and there has been very large buying of the new Japanese loan'.[9] Although British taxation later became a problem for foreign investors, and by the 1930s was a strong deterrent, it was of little consequence until Lloyd George more than doubled the rate of tax on larger incomes just before the war. Indeed, tax was far less of a block to investment in contemporary London than it was on the Continent.

Britons, too, bought securities through foreign markets. But before 1914 they had much less reason to do so than French investors who found it convenient (and cheaper) to subscribe in London to Egyptian, Russian and Japanese government bonds, to South African, 'Westralian' and Spanish mining shares. Germans bought 'Kaffirs' in London, and liked the government bonds of Brazil, China and Japan. Dutchmen used London as a kind of supermarket for Latin American securities. It is difficult to attach numbers to this phenomenon, and more difficult as the years passed. Buyers, sellers and securities moved freely in and out of London. There is no record of the ownership of nominee holdings (registered by foreigners in the names of British banks and others). By the mid twenties the greater part of foreign government securities and all foreign 'municipals' took the form of 'bearer' bonds (payable simply to 'bearer' without further specification),[10] and in the next decade bearer securities become the majority also for those issued by foreign railways and public utilities.[11] But they had been popular in London since well before the First World War, even as early as 1904 when foreign securities at last began to sell again in sizeable quantities. Bonds were 'nearly always to bearers' in the years before 1914, although debenture stocks were registered.[12]

No ready answer exists for complications such as these; impressions can be gathered from the comments of contemporaries, but little more. The problem is that London's open position as an international market – a market on which most major issues appeared – can and does lead to misunderstanding. A sufficiently dramatic example was the great Russian loan of 1909 (£56 million) of which £6 million was allotted to London. Sir George Paish described Russia as receiving £9.7 million in London subscriptions for 1909. No Russian railways of significance were listed in the *Stock Exchange Official Intelligence* for 1909, and in the absence of any evidence of spectacular contemporary borrowing for Russian municipalities, oil, or whatever, it is plain that the Paish figure for British subscriptions to Russia in 1909 included a full allowance of £6 million for Britons in the Government Loan, when it was known that some 80–85 per cent had actually been taken by France. Much the same had been true of 'British' investment in Russia for some time. Paish himself had reported in July 1907 that it was estimated on 'exceedingly good authority' that fully one half of London's allotted portion of the still greater Russian loan of 1906 – £13.1 million, out of a total of £85.3 million – had been bought by French investors.[13]

There is no need to labour the point. Foreigners bought and sold without impediment on the London Stock Exchange before the Great War, and the problem is to arrive at some realistic estimate of the portion within London issues for which they were responsible. Although it is feasible to develop a general average for all types of security, it must be said that the degree of British/Foreign ownership of London issues varied much between classes. In a category like 'British registered companies operating abroad', the *Economist* and Sir Robert Kindersley jointly estimated, from a sample of 532 companies over the full range, that only 7.7 per cent of share and loan capital in 1929 was held outside Britain: a minimum, since nominee and bearer securities actually held by foreigners made precision impossible.[14] For other categories, however, foreign ownership was proportionately much larger, and Kindersley's overall average for foreign holdings for the whole range of securities, 21 per cent in 1926, incorporates foreign ownership of only 1 per cent for utilities like waterworks and gas, but of nearly 60 per cent for banks and discount companies.[15]

Foreign government stock, only some 54 per cent of which had interest payable in London at the end of the 1920s,[16] was almost certainly held by foreigners to the extent of 30–40 per cent even before the First World War. Within the British Empire, Keynes concluded in 1909 (when confronted with an exaggerated account of the extent of British investment in Government of India securities) that 'we can no longer act on the assumption that the invested savings of the inhabitants of India are of no account'.[17] Obviously, Imperial government and municipal securities were better held in London than abroad; the percentage of foreign ownership before 1914 was small. But like others of their class, these drifted back to the domestic investor. Kindersley, writing near the end of the thirties, pointed out that for some countries more than 50 per cent of government sterling bonds were now held *out* of London; it had become a matter of public knowledge when publicity was given to the repurchase of low-priced, defaulted bonds during the depression of the 1930s. Kindersley added that it was not equally well known that over 11 per cent of Dominion government loans, and over 14 per cent of their municipal loans, were no longer owned in Britain.[18] As for equity holdings in firms, Lance Davis and Robert Huttenback estimate that around 16 per cent of foreign securities through London were foreign-held before the war; 8 per cent of Empire securities were taken by empire residents, and a further 2.5 per cent by foreigners.[19]

I am referring to Kindersley's estimates, for the 1920s and 1930s, simply because they are the best of their kind for the distribution of British and foreign ownership. Kindersley made a special point of this distinction, and returned to it at length in each of his articles. The formula he used was to calculate annual receipts from sinking fund and maturity payments on securities of foreign governments and companies operating abroad and listed on the London Stock Exchange. From these he isolated the amounts received by British and by foreign holders respectively. Kindersley's formula was not foolproof since it could not allow fully for securities held for foreign clients by British institutions. But it was more comprehensive than any before 1914 when Sir Robert Giffen had assumed that the capital of foreign issues brought out in Britain was 'wholly or mainly' held in Britain.[20]

Paish made no allowance for foreign ownership in his figures for 1907–8; he added a random, unexplained guess of 10 per cent, but only after the discussion that followed his paper.[21] Again without explanation, Imlah followed Paish.[22] Kindersley's estimates, since they are for the 1920s and 1930s, can serve only as an indicator; foreign buying of securities in London between the wars had declined, for reasons that included the deterrent of a now high rate for British income tax and the development of real competition from New York. But at its peak, before the war, foreign interest in the London market had been very high indeed. From June 1908 to June 1909, Paish reckoned that some 20 per cent of a total of £175.6 million in foreign and Empire issues in London was supplied by the Continent.[23] A leading article in the *Statist* of May 1910, almost certainly also by Paish (joint editor at the time), explained that over the past year Continental participation in London issues could well have been 25 per cent.[24] Two months later, when the market was particularly active, the *Statist* raised its estimate (for Continental subscriptions to new foreign issues in London over the previous six months) to as much as two-thirds.[25]

No solid evidence exists for the full extent of foreign participation. Paish suggested that in 1913, as a result primarily of the Balkan War, foreign purchasing of London issues was at an unusually low level. It is possible that London's experience for this particular year, more than usually important as marking the end of an era, has unduly influenced subsequent estimates; certainly Paish had detected a 'fair amount' as subscribed in 1911–12.[26] Over a longer and more representative period, bearing in mind the international character of the London market, the existence of so many branches and agencies of foreign and Imperial banks in the City and their role as issuing houses, underwriters and delegates on behalf of foreign clients, it would be no more than sensible to raise Paish's 10 per cent for the rate of overseas participation in London issues, to 20 per cent during the heavy overseas investment of 1908 to 1914. For the whole, less consistently strenuous span of fifty to sixty years leading up to the end of 1907 – the years covered in Paish's first paper – 15 per cent is probably enough.

## THE DISTRIBUTION OF 'PARTIALS'

A more specific and often misleading element in the whole problem of foreign ownership and the disposal of new issues was the distribution of 'partials'. These were loans for which a proportion was allocated to each of two or several international markets. They were common for large issues, but in practice recurred in the case of subscriptions for many smaller loans not sufficiently large themselves for subdivision. The entire amount of a foreign issue might be offered in London, but the whole or part might find its way abroad again.[27]

Paish claimed to have 'taken credit for only those portions of international loans, including railway issues, that had been subscribed for in this country'.[28] It is not possible to confirm this since Paish did not explain how he could have done so, and the remark was made simply in passing at the end of the discussion of his first paper to the Royal Statistical Society (1909). He made the same claim for his second paper; but apart from saying that he had made 'every allowance' for Continental participation, he did not specify what this might be.[29] Comparable sets of figures published annually in the

January issues of the *Economist* are supposed to have separated portions of international loans issued in London from those issued abroad, and Paish evidently intended to do the same. In the more obvious cases this was done, but even then there were many where no proper allowance was made. For the less obvious 'partials', and for smaller, unallocated loans, it is clear that neither Paish nor the *Economist* was able to make a realistic division between British and foreign subscriptions.

The general assumption at the time, at least among those not themselves directly engaged in the stock market, was that 'partials' should be divided, one half for London and the other for the Continent. C. K. Hobson, for one, thought so, to the extent of believing that an average of 50 per cent of 'partials' was both offered and *taken* in London.[30] More recently A. R. Hall has argued that a 50/50 division might actually *understate* British participation immediately before the war, just as it probably *overstated* London's share in the later decades of the nineteenth century; Matthew Simon agreed.[31]

It is true that some of the loans that reached London in the 1900s were split 50/50 between the London Stock Exchange and Continental bourses. An example of a straightforward 50/50 division can be cited as late as January 1911, when the Chilean Government issued a £5 million loan divided equally between Britain and Germany. But on the whole, 50/50 divisions were less common in the early twentieth century than they had been before. In earlier times, while the capacity of Continental investors was still relatively untried, a 50/50 division was natural. When the Imperial Government of China made its first serious application to European money markets in 1896, the business was shared equally between the Hong Kong & Shanghai Banking Corporation (for London) and the Deutsche-Asiatische Bank (for Berlin); the same formula was agreed for the rather larger (£16 million) Chinese Government loan of 1898.

The transition was illustrated by Japanese war finance during the Russo-Japanese War. Generally speaking, the Far East looked to London for government loans; the first Japanese War Loan of 1904 was shared equally between London and New York. It was so successful that the *Economist* regretted that the whole £10 million had not been offered in London, and part of the New York share was no doubt taken by Britons.[32] The second Japanese War Loan, for £30 million in March 1905, was again shared equally between London and New York. Subscriptions poured in from Paris and

Berlin, and a summer loan of a further £30 million was designed to be divided in three between London, New York and Berlin. Then, Paris finance houses showed themselves particularly anxious to take a leading part, and the Japanese 'conversion' loan of £25 million (December 1905) was distributed, £12 million to Paris, £6.5 million to London, and £3.25 million each to New York and Berlin.

It was in the interest of borrowers to shop around in European financial markets. A 50/50 formula continued to be applied where it was felt to be useful, and a large Japanese loan of 1907 (£23 million) was shared equally between London and Paris; it was a great success in both, although French subscribers were said to have taken a large share of London's 50 per cent. The city of Tokyo loan of 1912 offered only a third of its £9 million for subscription in London. But the Imperial Chinese Government loan of 1908 had been shared half and half by the Hong Kong & Shanghai Banking Corporation and the Banque de l'Indo-Chine. Some Argentine and Brazilian loans were issued half in London and half on the Continent in 1909. The city of Copenhagen, through Messrs Hambro of London, shared a small loan of £2.2 million equally between London and the Continent in 1910.

Loans issued simultaneously, without apportionment, were relatively common in the 1900s – Cuba in 1904, the American Telephone & Telegraph Co. in 1907, the National Railway (Brazil) in 1911, the city of Moscow in 1912, and the Chilean Government in 1913. No precise answer can now be given for Britain's share in each, and some issues, like those of the Government of India, were made totally in London. But it remains true that division and subdivision were more usual, especially for the years leading up to the First World War. 'It is very rare nowadays', said Mr Henry Beaumont in his criticism of Paish (1911)

> to get entirely to ourselves a loan of any importance; a large portion was always reserved for some foreign countries and he [Beaumont] did not think sufficient allowance had been made [by Paish] for the enormous transfer of securities from London to other European countries.[33]

Even if the nominal allocation of a 'partial' is known, the problem of the nationality of the actual buyer remains. I have referred to the first Japanese War Loan of 1904, when Britons in practice took a part of the 50 per cent allocated to New York. I have mentioned the

*Table* 2.1 'Partials' and the London market, 1905–14

| *Loan* | *Year* | *Quantity* (*£million*) | *Allocation (London)* (*£million*) |
|---|---|---|---|
| Japanese Government | 1905 | 25.0 | 6.5 (26.0%) |
| Russian Government | 1906 | 85.3 | 13.1 (15.4%) |
| Turkish Government | 1908 | 4.3 | 1.1 (25.6%) |
| Tientsin-Pukao Railway | 1908 | 3.0 | 1.1 (36.7%) |
| São Paulo (state) | 1908 | 15.0 | 5.0 (33.3%) |
| Russian Government | 1909 | 56.0 | 6.0 (10.7%) |
| Turkish Government (June) | 1909 | 4.3 | 1.1 (25.6%) |
| Turkish Government (Nov.) | 1909 | 6.4 | 2.0 (31.3%) |
| New York Telephone Co. | 1909 | 5.0 | 2.0 (40.0%) |
| Argentine Government | 1909 | 10.0 | 3.0 (30.0%) |
| Buenos Aires (province) | 1909 | 2.4 | 0.7 (29.2%) |
| Bulgarian Government | 1910 | 4.0 | 1.0 (25.0%) |
| Tientsin-Pukao Railway | 1910 | 3.0 | 1.1 (36.7%) |
| Hukuang Railway | 1911 | 6.0 | 1.5 (25.0%) |
| Greek Government | 1911 | 4.4 | 0.8 (18.2%) |
| São Paulo (city improvements) | 1911 | 2.0 | 0.8 (40.0%) |
| Argentine Ports (central) | 1911 | 3.3 | 1.1 (33.3%) |
| Brazil Railway | 1911 | 7.5 | 1.9 (25.3%) |
| Tokyo (city) | 1912 | 9.2 | 3.2 (34.8%) |
| Chinese Government | 1913 | 25.0 | 7.4 (29.6%) |
| Mexican Government | 1913 | 6.0 | 1.5 (25.0%) |
| Romanian Government | 1913 | 9.9 | 2.0 (20.2%) |
| Hungarian Government | 1914 | 21.0 | 3.0 (14.3%) |
| Greek Government | 1914 | 9.9 | 1.7 (17.2%) |
| Austrian Government | 1914 | 16.5 | 2.0 (12.1%) |
| Budapest (city) | 1914 | 6.6 | 1.0 (15.2%) |
| St Petersburg (city) | 1914 | 7.0 | 2.3 (32.9%) |

*Source*: *The Times*, *Economist*.

Brazil Railway issue of April 1911, where again Britons took a share nominally allocated to Amsterdam. More often it worked the other way. Frenchmen absorbed the British portion of the great Russian Government loans of 1906 and 1909, and Paris took up most of the London share of the Japanese loan of 1907. London's portion of Chinese Government loans after 1910 found a ready subscription among Continentals.

Table 2.1 shows a sample of 'partials' where London's share was less than 50 per cent; it is for the period of the revival of overseas investment after 1904. The percentages are not precise since the terms of each loan, published spasmodically by the financial press, were liable to swift, last minute alterations. Nevertheless, the table indicates what had come to be the case for 'partials'. The conclusion must be that their existence, the facts of their distribution, the experience of smaller issues sold in a single, international market (but in practice taken up elsewhere), make London issues an inadequate guide to the volume of *Britain's* foreign investment before 1914.

The point is not trivial. London's issues are those that are always quoted, yet London was the most international of security markets. Part-foreign applications in London in 1913, the year of Balkan disturbances, were as low as 12.4 per cent. In 1908 they had been 33.7 per cent, they were brought down to 16.9 per cent in 1909, up again to 25.6 per cent in 1910, and 31.3 per cent in 1911, and down to 24.8 per cent in 1912.[34] Large blocks of 'sterling' foreign loans were in fact issued in Paris, Berlin and Amsterdam before the war, and the bonds of Brazil and China were 'good examples of issues of which the proportion held abroad [was] conspicuously high in consequence'.[35]

## EXCHANGE RATES AND FLUCTUATIONS IN SECURITY PRICES

The other, major revision of Paish's figure arises more directly from the circumstance that he was calculating an aggregate of the investment of Britons overseas for the previous fifty to sixty years. As such, he had no reason to allow for what happened to the securities once issued and subscribed – not only subsequent losses, defaults, repatriation and redemption, but also the rise and fall of security prices and rates of exchange. Paish concerned himself exclusively with new issues. He may have been too sanguine and dismissive in doing so, and it must be said that the convenience of estimates limited to 'new issues' has influenced research ever since. But W. P. Kennedy is right to point out, in criticism both of Paish and of Matthew Simon, that it is 'not especially revealing over a long period simply to add the annual gross purchases of foreign securities without, at the same time, making an assumption about the disposition of present purchases'.[36]

This is a point to which I shall return. As Lenfant found, there was 'no way of measuring international sales and purchases of existing securities', at any rate for before the First World War. If a stock figure is genuinely intended, some attention should be paid, nevertheless, to what in modern jargon is known as the 'secondary market' – the buying and selling of second-hand securities, defaults, losses, repatriation and amortisation.

'New issues' remain the main point of focus. In an up-to-the-minute market like London, investment in new issues was for many reasons preferable to old, not least because issuing houses made sure that the terms they offered were attractive enough to compete, because payment was generally effected by instalments so spread as to recruit the 'man of moderate means', and because opportunities existed to mobilise the speculator. The comforting fact that emerged after a period of depression, said *The Times* in 1908, was that 'new issues will still be taken if only the jam be spread with sufficient generosity'.[37] But there are two phenomena, steady exchanges and stable prices, that simplify the task of adapting Paish's accumulated 'flow' figure to 'stock', and of allowing for movements on the secondary market.

The stability of currency exchanges in the century before 1914 is almost incredible to us today. War, political and economic mismanagement, the falling price of silver, and had their effect on the exchange rate. The Indian rupee fell almost continuously in line with the decline in the price of silver, from ten rupees to the £1 sterling in 1871 to sixteen in 1893, after which the British gold sovereign became legal tender at fifteen rupees so that the rupee remained at fifteen until 1914. The US dollar (and its associated currencies like the Mexican silver dollar and the Argentine gold peso) was accepted at a conventional rate of $5 to £1 in 1815 and was the same in 1914 (even if, in between, the American Civil War and the misfortunes of the Argentine paper peso and the Mexican silver dollar meant serious fluctuations). The French franc was twenty-five francs to £1 in the 1820s, and it still stood at twenty-five on the eve of the First World War.

Furthermore, we have learned to live with a history of changing prices on security markets, normally (but not always) a rise. In our own time the phenomenon is associated with inflation, but it is not to be expected from the stability in the exchanges just described. Even so, it is notably the case that security prices did *not* rise from the recovery of foreign investment in 1904 to the outbreak of war in 1914. Short-term fluctuations (the outcome of speculation, arbitrage, or whatever) were inevitable. But it is clear that prices in general remained remarkably stable, and even declined.

'A Stockbroker', writing in the *Economic Journal* of 1912, discovered that the average mean price of British railway ordinary stock had fallen from 154.76 in 1896 to 107.91 in 1911; by contrast, the ordinary stock of foreign and colonial railways had risen from 117.88 to 155.82.[38] His conclusions were suitably devastating (and often cited) in the tariff reform debate, but the size and quality of his sample – ten of the most profitable foreign/colonial railways (ordinary stocks and shares), compared with the ordinary stock of ten important, but not necessarily flourishing, home railways – are enough to cast doubt on what he said. It was a subject haunted by its political implications. A. W. Flux's paper to the Manchester Statistical Society (February 1911) concluded that the better class colonial and Indian securities had improved their position and price relative to home investment. But it was a dispute, as Avner Offer says, between optimists and pessimists. An optimist like Paish, with an interest in defending and promoting the virtues of foreign investment, felt that 'on balance the securities purchased [by Britons] ultimately possess a greater value than the price paid for them'.[39] More recently, Offer quotes Edelstein's work on 'realized rates of return' to confirm that the net returns to capital, both domestic and overseas, fell to a historically low level; the decline in 1909–13 was especially noticeable.[40]

The overall picture was not inviting. The evidence cited by Offer, both from the best index of the day (the *Banker's Magazine*) and from death duty statistics, confirms that for home and foreign investment together there had been stagnation and decline in prices overall since the mid-1890s.[41] For 1912, a busy year in foreign issues (although clouded by the onset of war in the Balkans), Thomas Skinner, editor of the *Stock Exchange Year Book*, reported that the higher classes of investment securities had suffered a further serious depreciation: colonial governments had fallen in a range of 1 to 7 per cent, practically without exception; the experience of foreign governments was even worse; railway properties had shared in the general decline.[42] Consols fell from $91\frac{3}{8}$ (highest) in 1904 to $75\frac{3}{4}$ (highest) in 1913, and this was reflected in the prices of all British domestic investment. To a lesser extent, the same could be said for foreign stocks and shares. With some exceptions, like Suez Canal £20 shares that stood at $178\frac{1}{2}$ (highest) in 1904 and had risen to 234 (highest) by 1913, or successful mining enterprises and tea and rubber plantations (until they fell into decline just before the War), the general tendency in representative securities was downward. It could be seen in the most popular of US railways, but it was the case for others too (Table 2.2).

*Table* 2.2 Foreign security prices in London, 1904 and 1913

| | *1904 (highest)* | *1913 (highest)* |
|---|---|---|
| India $3\frac{1}{2}$% stock | $107\frac{3}{8}$ | $91\frac{11}{16}$ |
| Transvaal 3% guaranteed | $99\frac{3}{8}$ | $91\frac{3}{4}$ |
| Canada 3% stock (regd.) | 99 | $88\frac{1}{2}$ |
| New South Wales 4% insurance stock | $109\frac{1}{2}$ | $102\frac{2}{3}$ |
| New Zealand 4% insurance stock | $107\frac{1}{2}$ | $102\frac{1}{2}$ |
| Argentine 5%, 1886–7 | $104\frac{3}{4}$ | $103\frac{1}{2}$ |
| Russian 4% railway bonds, series 1 | $98\frac{7}{8}$ | $91\frac{3}{4}$ |

*Source*: *Stock Exchange Official Intelligence* (1914) p. 1711.

J. H. Lenfant reported that for US 'rails', despite wild fluctuations, the average price after 1901 'remained approximately stable, with however a downward tendency after 1909', and where Lenfant found a marked rise (for railway securities in the British Possessions) he was using the unreliable 'political' figures of 'A Stockbroker'. Lenfant agreed that the general experience of security prices during his period was 'definitely unfavourable for the investor'.[43]

There is a see-saw in security prices that makes precise figures unattainable. Prices for the decade before the First World War were stable, probably on average slightly below the market rate of fifteen to twenty years before. They had risen handsomely in the boom of the late 1880s, but they were in decline in the early nineties and remained so until the revival of investor interest overseas in 1904; thereafter, prices were stagnant.

A 'stock' estimate must be taken, realistically, from the current market price. 'Flow' estimates, on the other hand, require the issue price, whether above or below nominal value. Lenfant believed that estimates based on nominal and market values of 'public' securities 'lead to broadly similar results',[44] and he may have been right. Domestic issues were normally at par. Some foreign issues were sold at a premium on par, others at a discount. Lenfant preferred nominal values, principally because of the irrationality of the market, up and down by turn, that so disturbed any consistent estimate,[45] and Kindersley found it better, whatever the disadvantages, to express his own estimated aggregates of British capital invested abroad in terms of nominal values; nominal values were superior to, and more convenient than, alternative methods of adopting market values or original costs. In most cases, Kindersley added, the issue price of debentures and shares did not differ greatly from the face value.[46]

Edgar Crammond, in his elaborate estimates for the end of 1906, found the market value of British investments abroad to be £2.7 billion, by contrast with a nominal value of £2.6 billion; the subsequent decline in market values must have narrowed the gap still further. There are dangers in arguing from individual, perhaps exceptional, cases. Crammond called attention to the contrast between the current market value of the securities of the stronger Latin American countries (Mexico, Brazil, Argentina, Uruguay, Chile and Cuba) where market and nominal values were close enough, and 'Peru and other South American Republics' where the nominal amount was £43.8 million and the market value less than half (£20.4 million): back in 1897 the nominal value for the securities of 'Peru and other South American Republics' was £39.1 million, and the market value £6.7 million![47]

## AMORTISATIONS AND REPAYMENTS

The problems of 'flow' estimates are many, but fortunately not mine. The cost of issue in London (although lower than it was on the Continent) included normal commissions, advertising, underwriting, overriding commission and stamp duty, amounting often to as much as 10 per cent of the issue itself and sometimes more. Underwriting, almost universal by the late 1900s as a promotional device even for the highest class of security, could cost as little as 1 per cent on Indian or Colonial Government bonds and 2 per cent on good foreign government issues. But the standard, conventional commission was 5 per cent, the overriding commission was 2½ per cent, and underwriting alone, on mining issues especially, might be charged at 25 to 50 per cent. An extreme case was the issue of £900 000 5 per cent first debentures for the Southern São Paulo Railway, February 1911, when the whole issue was underwritten at a commission of £45 500 in cash and £300 000 in fully paid shares; the bonds, said the *Economist*, 'cannot be recommended'.[48]

It can be imagined what sums like these can do to a 'flow' estimate, from which should also be subtracted 'vendors' shares and payments for goodwill and concessions (if the sellers were in the UK), the 'watering' of capital, and issues at large discounts on nominal prices. These all contributed to the creation of unreal sums substantially above the actual sums remitted. Paish allowed for some, but at this early stage in the 'flow' debate he had not allowed even for the counterflow of dividends and interest.

After the heavily (and deliberately) discounted issues of the mid-nineteenth century, when governments sold stock nominally at 3 per cent for reasons of national pride at a time when the ill-fame of their credit barely entitled them to 9 per cent, the practice declined; it still existed shortly before 1914, but it was far less common. Stock 'watering', on the other hand, was endemic in, say, US railway finance in the 1880s, and must have helped unnaturally to inflate subsequent estimates of 'flows'; 'scrip dividends' of up to 100 per cent were paid to shareholders on some of the largest railway lines. Edgar Crammond, who as Secretary of the Liverpool Stock Exchange had reason to know, reported two Spanish–American enterprises, the Nitrate Railways Company (Chile) and the United Railways of Havana, where 'watered' capital added over £2 million to the money supposedly subscribed by British investors.[49] For many reasons there was indeed 'a very big difference between the amount subscribed by British investors and that spent overseas . . . representing a transfer of ownership within Britain and not a capital investment of funds abroad'.[50] W. R. Lawson, although he did not entirely explain himself, must have been getting at much the same point when he complained, at the discussion of Paish's second paper (1911), that 'in every one of these transactions there was a great deal of finance; generally, there was quite as much credit as actual cash'.[51]

So much for 'flows'. A 'stock' estimate relates simply to the value of the investment at a particular time. The liability has been incurred whatever was 'liberated' on the way. 'Stock' requires sufficient allowance not only for what happened at or soon after the initial sale – the proportion bought and held in London by foreigners, 'partials', the shares of an issue taken by different Continental and US markets. It must take account also of what occurred subsequently to the securities, identified at the time of the estimate itself.

Paish, since he was adding up issues year by year, was not interested in what followed; he wanted merely to establish the amount of money invested by Britons overseas over the years. Default, loss, and (in the vocabulary of the present day) 'renegotiation', were not uncommon for government debt abroad in Paish's day, although less so than in the middle decades of the nineteenth century and perhaps more recently. By the end of the nineteenth century, and for many countries long before, repatriation was normal; government securities had become really attractive to domestic creditors, sometimes as required by the law, more often because they were reliable and instantaneously realisable at home and at fair prices. Railway securities too – the best, non-government investment of the day – were often as popular with the domestic investor. Allowance must be made, in addition, for sinking funds and maturities. Gustav Cassell saw little point in the citation of gross figures for new loans; these 'must be diminished by the presumably not unimportant and, as a rule, probably increasing regular amortisation of earlier loans'.[52] Theodor Gregory complained that 'the importance of the sinking-fund repayments has hitherto been neglected'.[53] Although both Cassell and Gregory were writing of the late 1920s, their point was as valid for before the war.

Sir Robert Kindersley was the first to make a real effort to allow for sinking funds and repayments; initially, these were 'the primary purpose of [his] inquiry'. In the exploratory, 'methodological' article that launched his annually repeated estimates, Kindersley explained how, in the course of his investigations of the destination of British savings (he was much associated with the National Savings Movement), he had been bothered by the fact that although estimates were available for British lending abroad, there seemed to be no reliable figures for the amounts repaid to investors by the operation of sinking funds and on maturity, both of which needed to be deducted from the totals. Kindersley had worked hard at it. He had made a systematic approach to the London banking agents of foreign governments, states/provinces, and municipalities. He had asked British companies operating abroad for information on the amount paid out by each for capital redemption, and the proportions assigned to persons resident in the UK. He mentioned quite specifically that the rate of repayment on capital invested overseas was the same before the war as that ascertained from his own investigations for 1926 and 1927, and he calculated repayments on

British accounts (sinking funds) to have amounted, in the single year 1913, to £11 million.[54]

Subsequently, Kindersley returned to the subject on several occasions. In his paper for 1929 he set out his conclusions for the percentage to be allowed for annual repayments. For foreign and colonial governments and corporations, he estimated annual repayments of 2.2 per cent; for companies operating abroad and registered in the UK, Kindersley's average was 1.23 per cent; for his third category, companies registered and operating abroad, his percentage was 1.1. The crude average over all three categories in 1929 was 1.5 per cent.[55] Lenfant, following the Kindersley formula, calculated repayments at £26 million in 1899, £36 million at the end of 1906, £45 million in 1910, and £25 million at the end of 1913. Over the fourteen years 1900 to 1913, Lenfant's estimate for total repayments amounted to £529 million, or a third of total current issues during the same period.[56] For the period that followed Paish's first figure (for the end of 1907), Lenfant felt that a reduction for repayments should be made of £200–300 millions in Paish's gross figures to the end of 1913.

A. R. Hall may be mistaken in referring to redemptions as 'relatively unimportant in total'.[57] W. A. Brown, when he considered the same problem in 1937, concluded like Kindersley that 'as a rough average over a long period of years it seems reasonable to suggest a rate of 1.5 per cent per annum for redemptions and repayments', to which he added a further 0.5 per cent for defaults and other capital losses.[58] E. Victor Morgan, while accepting the difficulty of comparing pre-war and post-war estimates of total investment, acknowledged that from Kindersley's estimates of sinking fund repayments for 1927 at £16.8 million, it seemed reasonable on the same basis to assume £15 million a year for his own period of research, 1914 to 1925.[59] Admittedly, maturities vary much for different types and qualities of investment – for railroads they averaged 29.8 years within the dependent Empire by comparison with 56.2 years for foreign countries.[60] An average is as much as can be expected. But these and the natural return of choice securities into domestic hands could make a great deal of difference to the final 'stock' figure.

## DEFAULTS AND LOSSES

Redemptions were only one side of the coin; the other was capital wastage and loss. Michael Edelstein has calculated, for Stock Exchange securities, a total net loss on overseas company insolvency and government default of some £500 million – £450 million for companies and £50 million for governments – over the whole period 1870 to 1913.[61] The assumption of equality for the rate both of home and overseas company insolvency that lies behind this calculation is curious, and has since been corrected.[62] The rate of insolvency for overseas companies must indeed have been higher, and the figure even larger than the £450 million proposed. But Edelstein has given us an estimate with which we can work, and it is likely to be more reliable than the convenient assumption in Imlah that capital losses can be ignored since they were more or less made up for by gains.[63]

It is a chastening thought that the collapse (in 1893) of US rails, the largest single element in Britain's non-government investment overseas, meant that 'within two years nearly one fourth of the total railway capitalisation of the United States had passed through the bankruptcy courts';[64] British holdings in US securities are said to have fallen by some 43 per cent as a direct result of the 1893 crisis, while in individual cases they dropped by as much as 50 to 70 per cent.[65]

I have referred already to the static market value of foreign securities before the war, and this was but one reflection of a history of default and loss. W. R. Lawson, in the discussion of Paish's 1911 paper, 'did not think that Mr Paish had made anything like sufficient allowance for what he [Lawson] might call the decay of our foreign investment . . . the wear and tear'.[66] A significant element of any figure, stock or flow, is the contrast between 'capital issues' and 'actual money calls'. The *Economist*, when it gave a figure for 'total cash subscription', meant the total cash requested at issue price. Paul Arndt calculated that for the years before the war (1904–13) there was a difference of £392 million between capital 'issues' and actual money calls. But he does not explain how he reached this figure, and he obviously had something far larger in mind.[67] New issues were almost invariably paid up by gradual instalments; delays and overlaps complicated the outcome; but if we take a period of years the difference should, in the main, iron itself out for a stock figure, although playing havoc with 'flows'. Paish's total 'subscriptions' for 1908–13 were £1.03 billion, whereas the actual money calls listed in the *Economist* for the same period amounted to £927 million.[68] If allowance is made for double-counting – for 'failures', 'false starts' and so forth – and for the circumstance that the difference between securities offered and money paid may look larger than it really was so long as underwriters were able to meet their obligations, it may be reasonable to say that actual money calls on company securities for the period 1908–14 lagged behind the 'capital issues' described by Paish and the *Economist* by an average of something like 5 per cent – a percentage that should apply both to 'stock' and 'flow' estimates.

'Underwriting' is a melancholy story. Generally speaking, it is an element in 'flow' estimates rather than 'stock'. All the same, the great increase, during the pre-war years, of the practice of underwriting issues on the London Stock Exchange does lead to problems for any stock figure that, in practice, has to be based on Paish. Since the sum involved, although substantial, is not enormous, and the arguments complex, I have consigned the whole subject to Appendix 1. All that needs to be said, at this point, is that Paish's assumption that an underwritten loan was *ipso facto* fully subscribed is inadequate. The truth, at this distance, is impossible to establish. But the argument put forward is sufficient to suggest that at least some allowance for underwriting failures should be included in both stock and flow figures for 1908–14.

## INVESTMENT ON EXCHANGES OTHER THAN LONDON'S

Until now I have taken account simply of the reduction of Paish's estimate. This is clearly substantial, perhaps to the extent, for portfolio investment, of almost a third. But additions must also be made to Paish if his figures are to be accepted as the base for a new estimate of the stock of British investment overseas in August 1914.

Paish's figures end on 31 December 1913, seven months before the outbreak of war. As it happened, the first months of 1914 were a period of feverish activity on the London Stock Exchange and these issues too must be taken into account. Matthew Simon calculates a total of £203 million for overseas 'money calls' in 1914.[69] This seems to be on the high side since the *Economist*'s figure for the total offered for subscription, new loans and new companies, British and overseas, 1 January to 1 August, was £172.2 million.[70] Investment on the Continent had fallen off remarkably in 1913, primarily because of the political fears and entanglements of the Balkan crisis. By contrast, Britain had 'gone on lending abroad on an enormous scale'.[71] This continued to be so for the first four months of 1914, although few government loans, after the Austrian Loan of April, were successful. Signs of recovery could be detected in May, but in June Russian loans were left on the hands of the underwriters; 88 per cent was returned of a substantial loan for the city of St Petersburg. Britain's domestic troubles in Ireland in the spring, together with increasing anxiety about political complications on the Continent, acted as a severe check both on British and Continental investors. The figure for new applications in the first half of 1914, although higher at £152.3 million than for similar periods since the boom of 1910, masked a serious decline after April.

Subject to the standard reductions, the capital issues up to August 1914 must therefore be added to Paish. Others too, already cited in Paish to the end of 1913, are either underestimated or simply ignored. Paish's allowance for 'direct' investment is certainly too low, but some varieties of securities not listed on the Stock Exchange also escaped identification within Paish's portfolio; this was the case with many US railway 'bonds' in the 1900s which by-passed the official Exchange and were sold direct, as it was for Argentine 'cedulas' – a generation of mortgage bonds distributed in large quantities in the late 1880s and sold easily both to British and Continental investors. Throughout the later decades of the nineteenth century, Scottish solicitors were actively engaged in raising money direct from their clients for investment overseas – cattle companies in the American West, tea estates in Ceylon, Australian finance and banking companies.[72] Just before the war, large institutional investors, such as insurance companies, were buying direct to escape the high minimum commission set for dealings on the London Stock Exchange. In the later decades of the nineteenth century a proportion of overseas institutions were accustomed to sell direct. John Bailey's account of the operations of the Australian Mercantile Land and Finance Company shows that it operated almost entirely with British capital, but that much of its capital was retailed directly through local agents in London, in the provinces, and in Scotland. Bailey's comment was that

> there existed outside the City a well-developed market for company securities which has been neglected in the study of British overseas investment because it has been assumed that

most issues were offered and subscribed through the issuing houses of the London Stock Exchange.[73]

This was certainly the case, but although noticeable the amount is unlikely to have been so large within the kind of figures we are now considering. Jacob Viner, in the course of his investigation of British investment in Canada (the most popular of destinations for this kind of investment in the years before 1914), calculated the sum of British small-lot purchases of Canadian securities, including bank shares, at £5 million from 1900 to 1913, to which he added another £7.8 million for private sales of securities by provincial and municipal governments and corporations.[74]

For similar reasons British provincial stock exchanges, cheaper and more flexible than London, were beginning to challenge what had been practically a monopoly of foreign issues through London. Paish took no account of any movement outside the London Stock Exchange. Again, the numbers involved are not large, even if they cannot be ignored. London, just before the war, was still overwhelmingly the market for foreign securities. The provincial exchanges dealt primarily with areas of transport, minerals, commerce and industry for which they could claim special knowledge and competence. Bristol and Cardiff took an interest in South Wales coal mines, the tinplate industry, and local dock and railway companies; Birmingham and Coventry were the headquarters of the bicycle, motor and engineering trades; Manchester dealt in the securities of weaving and spinning companies, Sheffield in the steel trade, Bradford in woollens and Burton-on-Trent in breweries. Dublin bought and sold all Irish securities, especially railways.

The Liverpool Stock Exchange was the most energetic in the promotion and sale of foreign securities – especially US and Argentine railways and South African mines, although the market for *government* issues remained limited to London. In 1914, Liverpool could hold its own against London within its special spheres of interest, and it is an indication of its power that it felt no need to fix a minimum price for 'Yankees' during the emergency that followed the declaration of war; Liverpool brokers felt confident that they could stabilise prices.[75] The two, big Scottish exchanges, Glasgow and Edinburgh, were markets for a group of Scottish-financed enterprises abroad that included land and plantation companies, insurance companies and investment trusts. Glasgow was known for speculation.

More significant was investment by Britons through stock exchanges abroad, and this too was not registered by Paish. British holdings on foreign exchanges fell far short of foreign holdings in London, and it is convenient but unrealistic to claim that they cancelled each other out.[76] Restrictions on dealings and heavy taxes made transactions on, say, German stock exchanges unattractive. Dr Bonn, even within a propaganda piece written during the war, acknowledged that British investments in pre-war Germany were 'overshadowed by the vast participation of German capital in flotations on the London Exchange . . . A large part of Germany's permanent investments, not only in British securities but also in other foreign securities, was made in London'.[77] Paris, in which British investors might also have been expected to buy and sell, was a disciplined and regulated market, unattractive to Britons; the government intervened to admit or reject securities, and a range of taxes on securities, domestic and foreign, made Paris several per cent more expensive than London.[78]

Nevertheless, convenience and tax evasion (on income tax and stamp duties) meant that a proportion of Britain's overseas investment found its way to foreign exchanges in the 'white' Dominions (such as those of Johannesburg and Melbourne) and on the Continent (at Paris and Berlin, but also at Amsterdam, Brussels, Antwerp, Frankfurt, Vienna, Basle, Geneva and Zurich). On the other hand, New York's 'new role in world finance', so much discussed in 1901, 'was forgotten by 1903 or 1907'.[79]

It may be that large British purchases on foreign exchanges in the 1920s have misled more recent opinion and disguised the peculiar advantages that London possessed as a market for international securities of every kind before the war. Kindersley reported, for the late 1920s, 'large and increasing investment by our nationals in United States securities issued and quoted only in New York'.[80] The impression that John Atkin gives (but also for New York's stock market boom of 1928–9), is of Britons as active in subscribing to new overseas issues in New York as foreigners in London.[81] Both were right, no doubt, but the circumstances were unusual and the same was not to be expected of stock markets before the First World War when London's pre-eminence was assumed.

## THE SECONDARY MARKET

'New issues' were particularly attractive to the British investor. But if Paish's figure for 'flows' are acceptable for new issues, they cannot ignore the secondary market if they are intended to represent 'stock'.

The difficulties are formidable. Paish's 1909 estimates (up to the end of 1907), if they can be taken as 'stock', might be said to allow to some extent for the movement of securities backwards and forwards on the 'secondary market'. His 'new issue' figures for 1908 to 1913 clearly do no such thing, and it is not obvious that a 'stock' figure can ever be entirely conclusive on the point. Securities on the secondary market were bought, sold, rebought and resold. Investors transacted their business as they pleased; speculative dealings cannot necessarily be distinguished from genuine investment; arbitrage operations (sales of securities between exchanges to take advantage of marginal price differentials) kept securities moving daily.

Many cases existed for which such movements were not recorded, but really large transactions caught the eye of City journalists. US 'rails' were the largest single class of foreign security on the London market. As an example of what could happen, I have tried in Chapter 6 to show the outcome of the decline in British ownership from over £600 millions in the late 1880s and early nineties to a quarter of that sum at the turn of the century. US railway securities were repurchased on a large scale during the boom of 1909–11 so that just before the war Britain's stock, although perhaps only half as much as it had been at the peak, was back at the formidable sum of £300 million. These transactions, naturally, were unrecorded in Paish's flow figure for 'new issues'.

Bearing in mind the volume of business – sales, losses and defaults, repatriation and maturities – it is unlikely that British operations on the secondary market, by contrast with 'new issues', would actually have shown much of a net increase, more probably the reverse, for the decade before 1914. Indeed, in an Exchange as obsessed with 'new issues' as London, the secondary market was employed rather for disposal than acquisition; disposal of old holdings supplied the funds to respond to tempting offers of new. The secondary market for existing securities was most active on the exchanges of Continental Europe and the United States; London was the core of the new issue market, in contact with the more distant customers overseas. Charles Kindleberger explains how the majority of capital flows in London were new issues.[82] Movements of securities on the new issue market, for Michael Edelstein, were 'overwhelmingly the most important' element in any correct total of UK holdings; as such, they are a 'good proxy for the movement, timing and, to a lesser extent, the amplitude' of subsequent sales, purchases and resales.[83]

## 'DIRECT' INVESTMENT

It is not clear that transactions on the 'secondary market' can be expected to supplement and increase Paish's 'new issues'. The emphasis is rather the other way, and I have made some allowance for this already when discussing repatriation, loss and default.

There are, however, other cases where some addition might naturally be expected to Paish's total. One might be the sum placed in reserve by British companies operating abroad, although in Kindersley's view, and correctly, reserves were reserves and might be drawn on – they could not be regarded as increased capital or income.[84] The area in which Paish's overall figure for British investment should be challenged most legitimately, in an upward direction, is his estimate for 'direct' investment, 'hopelessly neglected' as it has been, says Mira Wilkins, 'in studies of capital flows'.[85] And direct investment, in the simpler definition current in Paish's day, was investment that did not touch a stock exchange.[86]

The London Stock Exchange and the market in new issues have attracted most attention, quite naturally, for stock and flow estimates before the First World War. But new issues were 'only a part of a much wider whole in which must be included loans, mortgages, and other types of private financing which seldom appear in statistics and about which little information is available'.[87] 'Much wider" is misleading; Grant meant wider in range and diversity rather than in quantity. Portfolio investment in new issues remained the most important by a long way. Lenfant refers to 'the unknown and often unknowable importance of private investment and of ploughed back profits', amounting probably to between 10 and 20 per cent of the publicly issued capital. He was hedging his bets between Edgar Crammond's 13 per cent (in 1910), Paish's 18.5 per cent (in his first paper), Paish's subsequent reduction to about 10 per cent (1911 and 1914 papers), and Jacob Viner's much higher proportion of 22 per cent for British direct investment in Canada, averaged over the years 1900 to 1913.[88] After the war, Sir Robert Kindersley, while claiming 'no great degree of accuracy for this figure', put total British investment abroad in unquoted securities, property, etc. at £300 million, and he later increased his estimate for the second half of the 1930s, after much buying by Britons of unlisted US and Canadian stock, to £400 million.[89] Over the whole period 1870–1936, Frankel is quoted with approval as calculating Britain's private, direct investment in British Africa (including South Africa) at 8.7 per cent of publicly issued capital.[90]

The disparity of such estimates is not as extraordinary as it might seem. The scope of direct investment changed very much from year to year and from place to place. It was more likely between neighbours, over tariff walls. Buckley calculates that the extension of US industry over the Canadian frontier accounted for 'well over half of the $800 million of American investment up to 1914'; US direct investment in Canada had reached $2 billion by 1930.[91] Publicly issued capital was recorded and classified; it therefore attracted attention. Yet for even the largest of industrial enterprises, shares in Standard Oil of New Jersey were not quoted on any stock exchange before 1920, or, in the case of the Ford Motor Company before 1955. Paish's estimate for British investment in China at the end of 1913 was only £43.9 million; his figure naturally was for portfolio investment (new issues). C. F. Remer, who incorporated within his own estimate resident British business in Hong Kong and China (particularly in Shanghai), reached a total of over £120 million, almost three times the figure in Paish. As Remer said in defence of the higher amount, he had included all income-producing holdings in China that were in the hands of foreigners, whether they lived in China or abroad: 'the definition of foreign investments used here is not usual but it is the only one which is appropriate to the Chinese situation'.[92] His distinction finds echoes in Viner's work on Canada before the war, and in Pandit's on India for the same period.[93]

The £300 million estimated by Paish as Britain's direct investment overseas at the end of 1910 was, as Keynes pointed out, a perfectly arbitrary estimate for which no adequate reason had been given.[94] When Paish carried through an untouched £300 million for direct investment at the end of 1913, three years later, it might be imagined – perish the thought – that he was merely rounding off his £3.7 million portfolio to a neat £4 billion portfolio and direct.

Unfortunately no figure makes much sense. At what point does the 'direct' investment of a British immigrant in farm, city or industry become the 'domestic' capital of the country in which he settles? What must be allowed for property abroad owned by private individuals resident in the United Kingdom? What is to be done with the £25 per head that Noel Butlin accepts as a realistic level for 'migrants' capital' brought into Australia from the United Kingdom?[95] How can one account for the capital and reinvested profits of a British firm resident and trading almost entirely abroad, like Jardine Matheson and Butterfield & Swire in Shanghai and Canton, Balfour Williamson and Duncan Fox in Santiago (Chile), the great 'agency houses' of South and South East Asia, the overseas banks (the Bank of London and South America, the Hong Kong & Shanghai Bank, the Chartered Bank of India, Australia & China, the Imperial Bank of Persia)? In part these businesses appeared on the London capital market, but Keynes calculated for India in 1910 that British companies not quoted on any English exchange represented an aggregate capital of £50 million,[96] much of which was supplied by resident Britons but later shipped back as personal wealth to the UK.[97] John Stopford has called attention to 'expatriate' investment, by which he means the money raised from the home country by emigrant entrepreneurs; 'most probably', he says, 'there were thousands of "expatriate" British firms before 1914'.[98]

No doubt some formula can be invented to cover each of these, but it would be an exercise in theory, a 'model' for which supporting figures no longer exist. Even if some evidence could be gathered three-quarters of a century after the event, there would be much unavoidable overlap. Paish himself had given one estimate (£500 million) for 1907–8,[99] and two others (both £300 million) for the end of 1910 and 1913.[100] Edgar Crammond allowed about £450 million for non-portfolio investment at the end of 1910, which he defined as

> British capital employed in the shipping industry and by banking, insurance, and other companies . . . private investments of British subjects in land and buildings etc., in the Colonies and in foreign countries . . . large sums employed by the great private British finance and mercantile houses in financing foreign trade, etc.[101]

Both Crammond and Paish refer to short-term credit, or the financing of trade, as incorporated within their estimates for direct investment; Paish thought it to be the equivalent of about £100 million.[102] Much capital was tied up in London's short-term credit to foreigners before 1914. The *Economist* estimated the average value of 'foreign bills outstanding' at £336 million in 1913–14,[103] and the figure that most people seem to have in mind for bills of exchange drawn on London just before the war is £350 million, almost entirely connected with international trade.[104] But much of this business was not British at all. Although bills on London were real enough, a high proportion was transacted from the imported, capital resources of foreign branch banks in London (the Deutsche Bank, the Dresdner Bank and the Diskonto Gesellschaft in particular, although colonial and Dominion banks and the banks of France, Italy, Holland, Belgium and Austria–Hungary were well represented).[105] Thomas Balogh suggested that foreign deposits in London banks before the war accounted for about two-thirds of acceptance credits outstanding for foreigners,[106] and the foreign contribution is likely to have been even greater; as Kindersley found for his own merchant bank (Lazards), foreign deposits lent to the discount market, invested in Treasury Bills or otherwise, were *equal* to the bills drawn.[107] Britons too made substantial deposits in foreign branch banks in London, but David Williams may be near the mark when he estimated Britain's actual contribution to credit in overseas trade at only £130 million in 1914.[108]

If all of this is taken into account and some allowance is made for direct investment in 1914, Paish's estimate of £300 million is too low. It is reasonable to retrieve Paish's first thoughts, and to return to an estimate of £500 million as a minimum for Britain's 'direct' investment abroad as it stood in the summer of 1914.

## REVISIONS AND A NEW STOCK FIGURE

Where does this leave us? I have argued that we must start from Paish's figure of £3.7 billion for 31 December 1913, a figure that may serve, albeit imperfectly, as a kind of stock estimate for the end of 1907 to which was added an aggregate of capital issues for the years 1908 to 1913.

My first suggestion is a large reduction of Paish's total to allow for foreign purchases on British exchanges. Paish's estimate for the end of 1907 contained no such reduction, and his numbers for aggregated investment before 1908 should therefore be reduced by 15 per cent. From 1908 to 1913 Paish allowed 10 per cent, plus another 2 per cent for miscellaneous items. I propose to allow a further 8 per cent for 1908–13 to bring the total to 20 per cent for the foreign share during what had become the peak period of foreign activity on London's international market. Together, the reduction amounts to £487 million.

'Partials' have been overestimated by Paish, and the formula dividing partials 50/50 between London and other international markets is not sustainable. An exact figure is impossible, and I am assuming that Paish's estimate up to the end of 1907 at least reflects a genuine division. However, for the years 1908 to 1913, during which some of the biggest of 'partial' loans were made on international markets, when there was much 'drift' of securities generally, and when London's share so often passed to the Continent, it would be reasonable to allow a reduction of Paish's total by £150 million (15 per cent).

Repatriation and redemption are reflected to some extent in the disappearance of indebtedness even before Paish reached his total from the figures available for the half century before 1907. But the figures he actually employed did not take account of securities now held by foreigners that had been bought originally by Britons and sold subsequently on the secondary market. The debt outstanding as reported in the *Stock Exchange Intelligence*, and calculated by Paish as British, included much that had in practice long ceased to be owned in Britain. Bearing in mind the return more particularly of government and railway securities to the domestic investor, it might be supposed that under this head Paish's estimate for *British* holdings is overestimated to the extent of at least 5 per cent – that is, by £135 million.

Paish's total for 1908–13 – the accumulation of new issues on the London Exchange – naturally took no account of repatriation and redemption. If, in order to arrive at a stock figure, we were to take Kindersley's formula of 1.5 per cent applied annually for six years, the amount to be removed from Paish would be a further £16 million.

Taken for the whole period 1870–1914, Edelstein estimates losses and defaults of £450 million for companies and £50 million for governments. Prices for securities of all kinds were relatively static for the decades after 1890–1, but losses must to some extent have been offset by gains so that a maximum of £350 million should be deducted from Paish's 'flow' figures for losses and defaults.

If £100 million were removed from Paish's totals for failed issues and for the distortions of 'underwriting' incorporated in his total, and £30 million for the difference between capital issues and actual money calls on private issues for 1908–13, then the total reductions on Paish's estimates amount to £1.268 billion.

On the other hand, what I have been trying to establish is a stock figure for British investment right up to the outbreak of the First World War. Paish's annual totals were for new issues on the London Stock Exchange to 31 December 1913. If these are to be taken to August 1914 then another £70 million should be added for colonial and foreign issues on London, incorporating a reduction of some 45 per cent on the gross figures for foreign ownership, repatriation, redemption, failures, loss, and the disparity between issues and money calls.

Paish made no allowance for British investment overseas either through domestic exchanges other than London or through foreign and Empire bourses. I have explained why I think that such investment is unlikely to have been large. But it would be reasonable to add £65 million, allowing both for direct investment until August 1914 and for a portion of provincial investment incorporated in Paish's figures to the end of 1907. I have added another £50 million for securities that were sold direct (and thus unrecorded on any exchange).

Finally, the largest addition that I suggest is certainly to be found in direct investment. Like Paish I have incorporated £100 million of short-term finance into 'direct' investment. As it stands, at £300 million for all direct investment, Paish's estimates are too small. I have added another £200 million, and brought the figure back to the £500 million estimated in Paish's first paper of 1909.

Taking reductions and additions together, my estimate for British portfolio investment abroad, 1 August 1914, is £2.6 billion (incorporating items not included in Paish, i.e. new issues for 1914, unregistered securities, and securities bought on British and foreign exchanges other than London's). I have raised Paish's £300 million for direct investment to £500 million. Consequently, I suggest that the stock of British investment overseas on the eve of the First World War was more likely to have been somewhere in the region of £3.1 billion, portfolio and direct. The new figures are summarised in Table 2.3.

*Table* 2.3 Britain's stock of investment overseas, 31 July 1914 (£ billions, rounded to the nearest million)

| | A portfolio | B direct | total (A+B) |
|---|---|---|---|
| *Paish's estimates for 31 December 1913* | *£3.715* | *£0.300* | *£4.015* |
| PORTFOLIO INVESTMENT | | | |
| *Reductions* | | | |
| Foreign share of London subscriptions, 1908–13 | £0.083 | | |
| Foreign share of London subscriptions to 31 December 1907 | £0.404 | | |
| Partials and 'drift' | £0.150 | | |
| Unidentified foreign repurchases on the secondary market to 31 December 1907 | £0.135 | | |
| Repatriation and redemption, 1908–13 | £0.016 | | |
| Losses and defaults 1870–1914 | £0.350 | | |
| Failed issues and deficiencies in underwriting 1908–14 | £0.100 | | |
| Issues less money calls (companies) 1908–13 | £0.030 | | |
| | −£1.268 | | |
| *Increases* | | | |
| New issues (colonial and foreign) 1 Jan. to 31 July 1914 | £0.070 | | |
| British purchases of securities in exchanges other than London | £0.065 | | |
| Purchases of unregistered securities | £0.050 | | |
| | +£0.185 | | |
| DIRECT INVESTMENT | | | |
| *Increase* | | | |
| | | +£0.200 | |
| BRITAIN'S STOCK OF INVESTMENT OVERSEAS 31 JULY 1914 | £2.632 | £0.500 | £3.132 |

## Notes

1. *Statist*, 20 April 1907, p. 774.
2. J. M. Keynes, 'War and the Financial System, August 1914', *Economic Journal*, XXV (Sept. 1914) pp. 461–2.
3. Professor W. A. Brown's report to the United States Research Bureau, quoted in 'British Capital Abroad', *Economist*, 20 Nov. 1937, p. 362. The share calculated by Brown for 'British' investment abroad was 22.4 per cent in 1905–9 and 18.8 per cent for 1910–14.
4. Cornelius Rosenraad (President of the Federation of Foreign Chambers of Commerce) speaking in the discussion on Paish (1909) pp. 484–5.
5. 'New Year Prospects', *Statist*, 28 Dec. 1907, p. 1212.
6. *Statist*, 20 April 1907, p. 774.
7. Ibid., 6 June 1908, p. 1121.
8. A. Emil Davies, *Investments Abroad* (Chicago, 1927) p. 105.
9. *Statist*, 13 April 1907, p. 722.
10. Davies, *Investments Abroad*, p. 64.
11. Sir Robert Kindersley, 'British Overseas Investments in 1933 and 1934', *Economic Journal* (Sept. 1935) p. 450. Kindersley's articles in the *Economic Journal* are referred to hereafter simply under surname, month and year of publication.
12. Charles Duguid, *The Stock Exchange* (London, 1904) p. 88; Duguid was City Editor of the *Morning Post*. Hartley Withers, *Stocks and Shares* (London, 1917 edn) p. 47.
13. *Statist*, 20 July 1907, p. 106.
14. *Economist*, 1 March 1930, p. 453, and ibid., 22 March 1930, p. 634.
15. Kindersley (March, 1929) p. 11.
16. Ibid. (Sept. 1931) p. 372.
17. Letter to the editor of the *Economist*, printed 8 May 1909, pp. 983–4.
18. Kindersley (Dec. 1938) p. 612.
19. Lance Davis and Robert A. Huttenback, 'The Export of British Finance: 1865–1914', *Journal of Imperial and Commonwealth History*, XIII, 3 (May 1985) p. 33.
20. R. Giffen, 'Recent Accumulations of Capital in the United Kingdom', in his *Essays in Finance* (1880) p. 171.
21. Paish (1909), discussion p. 490.
22. Albert Imlah, *Economic Elements in the Pax Britannica* (Cambridge, Mass., 1958) pp. 78–9. Brinley Thomas also adopted the Paish formula in his 'The Historical Record of International Capital Movements to 1913', in J. H. Adler (ed.), *Capital Movements and Economic Development* (New York, 1967) p. 6.
23. George Paish, 'The Advantages of the Export of Capital by the Older Countries', *Statist*, 1 January 1910, pp. 17–21. This was a reprinted paper first delivered to the 'Finance Forum' of New York, 15 Dec. 1909.
24. 'Our Capital Investments', *Statist*, 7 May 1910, pp. 993–4.

25. 'Our Investments of New Capital', *Statist*, 9 July 1910, pp. 67–9.
26. 'Our Great Savings', *Statist*, 3 Jan. 1914, p. 20.
27. J. M. Keynes, 'Great Britain's Foreign Investments', *New Quarterly*, February 1910, reprinted in Elizabeth Johnson (ed.), *The Collected Writings of John Maynard Keynes*, vol. XV (1971) p. 58.
28. Paish (1909) discussion p. 484.
29. Paish (1911) p. 171.
30. C. K. Hobson, *The Export of Capital* (1914) pp. 181, 218.
31. A. R. Hall, 'A Note on the English Capital Market, as a Source of Home Investment before 1914', *Economica*, n.s. XXIV (1957) p. 62 (fn. 2), and Simon, 'The Pattern of New British Portfolio Investment, 1856–1914', in Adler, *Capital Markets*, p. 54.
32. 'The Financial Position of Japan', *Economist*, 7 May 1904, p. 823.
33. Paish (1911), discussion p. 193.
34. 'The Capital Market', *Economist*, Commercial History and Review of 1913, p. 418.
35. Kindersley (Dec. 1936) p. 647.
36. W. P. Kennedy, 'Foreign Investment, Trade and Growth in the United Kingdom, 1870–1913', *Explorations in Economic History*, 11, 4 (Summer 1974) p. 442.
37. *The Times*, 3 April 1908, Financial and Commercial Supplement, p.le. J. F. Wheeler described the technical attraction of 'new issues' in his general book on *The Stock Exchange* (n.d. ?1913) p. 78.
38. A Stockbroker, 'The Depreciation of British Home Investments', *Economic Journal*, XXII, 86 (June 1912) pp. 220, 223–4.
39. Paish (1909) p. 473.
40. Avner Offer, *Property and Politics 1870–1914: Landownership, Law, Ideology and Urban Development in England* (Cambridge, 1981) p. 104.
41. Ibid., 'Empire and Social Reform: British Overseas Investment and Domestic Politics, 1908–1914', *Historical Journal*, 26, 1 (1983) pp. 129–30; also his *Property and Politics*, pp. 111, 146.
42. T. Skinner, *The Stock Exchange Year Book for 1913* (1913) p. v.
43. J. H. Lenfant, 'British Capital Export, 1900–1913' (unpublished Ph.D. thesis, University of London, 1949) pp. 264–6.
44. Ibid., p. 67.
45. Ibid., pp. 48–9.
46. Kindersley (Sept. 1935) pp. 439–40.
47. E. Crammond, 'British Investments Abroad', *Quarterly Review*, 412 (July 1907) p. 249.
48. *Economist*, 11 Feb. 1911, p. 275.
49. Crammond, 'British Investments Abroad', p. 254.
50. Hall, 'A Note on the English Capital Market', p. 63.
51. Paish (1911), discussion p. 191.
52. Cassell, 'The Utility of Foreign Investment', in G. Cassell *et al.*, *Foreign Investments* (Chicago, 1928) p. 55.
53. T. Gregory, 'Foreign Investments and British Public opinion', in ibid., p. 136.
54. Kindersley (March 1929), pp. 9–11, 22. This is the first article of the series, in which he explained his approach to the whole problem.

55. Ibid. (Sept. 1931) pp. 378, 381.
56. Lenfant, 'British Capital Export', pp. 62–3.
57. Hall (ed.), *The Export of Capital from Britain, 1870–1914* (1968) p. 13.
58. In 'British Capital Abroad', *Economist*, 20 Nov. 1937, p. 360.
59. E. V. Morgan, *Studies in British Financial Policy, 1914–25* (1952) p. 323.
60. L. E. Davis and R. A. Huttenback, 'Export of British Finance, 1865–1914', p. 74, fn. 16.
61. M. Edelstein, 'Realized Rates of Return on UK Home and Overseas Portfolio Investment in the Age of High Imperialism', *Explorations in Economic History*, 13 (1976) p. 298.
62. Ibid., 'Foreign Investment and Empire, 1860–1914', in Roderick Floud and Donald McCloskey (eds), *The Economic History of Britain since 1700*, vol. II (Cambridge, 1981) pp. 84–5.
63. Imlah, 'British Balance of Payments and Export of Capital, 1816–1913', *Economic History Review*, 2nd ser. V, 2 (1952) p. 226, and in chapter III of *Economic Elements in the Pax Britannica*. Paish argued that losses were more than amply compensated for by gains: Paish (1909) p. 473.
64. Alexander D. Noyes, *Forty Years of American Finance* (New York, 1909) p. 218.
65. *Statist*, quoted by W. Turrentine Jackson, *The Enterprising Scot: Investors in the American West after 1873* (Edinburgh, 1968) p. 251.
66. Paish (1911), discussion p. 192.
67. P. Arndt, 'Neue Beiträge zur Frage der Kapitalanlage im Ausland', *Zeitschrift für Socialwissenschaft*, N.F., VI (1915) p. 305.
68. 'The Capital Market', *Economist*, Commercial History and Review of 1913, 21 Feb. 1914, p. 418.
69. M. Simon, 'Pattern of New British Portfolio Foreign Investment', p. 40, fn. 1.
70. *Economist*, 1 Aug. 1914, p. 236.
71. *Statist*, 17 Jan. 1914, p. 104.
72. J. D. Bailey, *A Hundred Years of Pastoral Banking: A History of the Australian Mercantile Land and Finance Company 1863–1963* (Oxford, 1966) p. 66.
73. Ibid., pp. 61–2. Also Bailey, 'Australian Borrowing in Scotland in the Nineteenth Century', *Economic History Review*, 2nd ser. XII, 2 (1959) pp. 268–79, and Eric Richards, *Australia and the Scottish Connection, 1778–1914* (London, 1985) pp. 146–7.
74. J. Viner, *Canada's Balance of International Indebtedness, 1900–1913* (Cambridge, Mass., 1924) pp. 122, 126.
75. W. A. Thomas, *The Provincial Stock Exchanges* (1973) p. 190.
76. As does J. Fred Rippy, *British Investments in Latin America, 1822–1949* (Minneapolis, 1959) p. 67.
77. M. J. Bonn, 'The Nationalization of Capital', in E. M. Patterson (ed.), *America's Changing Investment Market* (Annals of the American Academy of Political and Social Science, Philadelphia, 1916) pp. 256–7. Bonn was a professor at the University of Munich.
78. Yves Guyot, 'The Amount, Direction and Nature of French

Investments', in ibid. pp. 38, 41–7. Guyot was editor of the *Journal des Economistes*.

79. Alexander D. Noyes, *The War Period of American Finance, 1908–1925* (New York, 1926) p. 127.
80. Kindersley (June 1930) p. 176.
81. J. M. Atkin, 'British Overseas Investment, 1918–1931' 'Ph.D. thesis, University of London, 1968) p. 225. He was quoting a memorandum dated 12 Nov. 1928.
82. C. Kindleberger, 'International Propagation of Financial Crises: The Experience of 1889–93', in Wolfram Engels *et al.* (eds), *International Capital Movements, Debt and Monetary System* (Mainz, n.d.) p. 219.
83. Edelstein, 'The Determinants of UK Investment Abroad, 1870–1913: The US Case', *Journal of Economic History*, XXXIV, 4 (Dec. 1974) p. 991.
84. Kindersley (Dec. 1936) p. 660.
85. Mira Wilkins, 'Modern European Economic History and the Multinationals', *Journal of European Economic History*, 6, 3 (Winter 1977) p. 584. This is a pioneering and bibliographical article of some importance. Professor Wilkins has taken particular care to isolate direct investments (using the modern definition); she has published much already on the subject, and is publishing more.
86. The more complicated definition of direct investment now current, as I explained in the previous chapter, is investment controlling 10 per cent (and in some definitions up to 30 per cent!) of equity in a business.
87. A. T. K. Grant, *A Study of the Capital Market in Britain from 1919–36* (edn 1967) pp. 120, 123.
88. Lenfant, 'British Capital Export', pp. 46, 60. Viner's calculations are given in his *Canada's Balance of International Indebtedness*, pp. 123–6: as they deal with a 'white' Dominion in the midst of an unprecedented boom in British investments and immigration, the unusually large element of direct investment is understandable (and not representative).
89. Kindersley (Dec. 1936) p. 653; ibid. (Dec. 1937) p. 656 fn. 1; ibid. (Dec. 1939) p. 693.
90. D. K. Fieldhouse, 'The Economic Exploitation of Africa: Some British and French Comparisons', in Prosser Gifford and Roger Louis (eds), *France and Britain in Africa: Imperial Rivalry and Colonial Rule* (Newhaven, Conn., 1971) p. 655, table 8.
91. Kenneth Buckley, *Capital Formation in Canada, 1896–1930* (Toronto, 1955) p. 66.
92. C. F. Remer, *Foreign Investments in China* (New York, 1933) pp. 63–76.
93. J. Viner, *Canada's Balance of International Indebtedness*, pp. 120–6, and Y. S. Pandit, *India's Balance of Indebtedness 1898–1913* (1937) pp. 109–31.
94. Paish (1911), discussion p. 195. Keynes was referring to Paish's remarks on p. 187.
95. N. G. Butlin, *Australian Domestic Product, Investment and Foreign Borrowing, 1861–1938/9* (Cambridge, 1962) p. 453.
96. J. M. Keynes, 'Great Britain's Foreign Investment', p. 47.

97. This is well documented by now, and much has been published, notably by A. K. Bagchi. Bagchi's *Private Investment in India 1900–1939* (Cambridge, 1972) is particularly valuable.
98. J. Stopford, 'The Origins of British-Based Multinational Manufacturing Enterprises', *Business History Review*, XLVIII, 3 (Autumn 1974) pp. 305, 307.
99. Paish (1909) discussion pp. 490–1.
100. Paish (1911) p. 187 and Paish (1914) p. v.
101. Crammond, 'British Investment Abroad', p. 46.
102. Paish (1909) discussion p. 490.
103. Quoted by Lenfant, 'British Capital Export', p. 75.
104. H. S. Foxwell, *Papers on Current Finance* (1919) pp. 3, 13 (a reprint of an article published originally in the *Economic Journal* of Dec. 1915), but see also Morgan, *Studies in British Financial Policy*, p. 332.
105. The point is discussed helpfully by Lawson, *British War Finance*, pp. 9, 40–51, 140–6.
106. T. Balogh, *Studies in Financial Organization* (Cambridge, 1947) p. 248.
107. Minutes of Evidence, *Report of the Committee on Finance and Industry*, vol. I (HMSO, 1931), Q.1157.
108. Williams, 'London and the 1931 Financial Crisis', *Economic History Review*, 2nd ser. XV (1963) p. 515, fn. 1.

# 3 Politics, Propaganda and Numbers

I mentioned in Chapter 1 how Paish's estimates entered conventional wisdom by way of the Chancellor of the Exchequer, the Board of Trade, the League of Nations, the Royal Institute of International Affairs and the United Nations. In Chapter 2 we have seen how vulnerable these numbers turned out to be. I should now explain the peculiar circumstances that persuaded a majority of Paish's contemporaries to accept his estimates and even to welcome them. Keynes, who in a few words was virtually to demolish the argument in Paish's second paper (1911), had been glad enough to use the estimates from Paish's first paper when they were needed to establish his point against Fair Traders.[1] The convenience of a long run of figures, whether from Paish or from Imlah, has been much appreciated ever since.

Eugene Staley, in his efforts to make sense of the figures that led up to the Slump, mentioned the immense range of estimates with which he had dealt, the extreme unreliability even of the best, and the variable quality of the estimates for foreign capital holdings by the time he himself was writing:

> Some have been arrived at in the course of estimates of national wealth or income, others in the discussion of foreign trade history, others to be used as propaganda for larger navies, and many with reference to post-War problems connected with international debts and reparations.[2]

This was precisely the case, and it was one of the phenomena of the time that, in the years before the war, all manner of interests, competing or complementary, took but one position: the great size of Britain's investments overseas. Then, during the war itself, propaganda that was designed to establish the strength of the rival Empires, British, French and German, reproduced the biggest figures that could be found to prove each nation's claim. It was no wonder that the quest for a reliable figure was at first postponed, and then ultimately forgotten.

## TARIFF REFORM AND THE FIGURES

The debate on tariff reform – Fair Trade against Free Trade – had interested economists and politicians from well before the turn of the century. The National Fair Trade League, in emulation of Germany's Zollverein, had promoted preferential tariffs back in the 1880s. The first Imperial Conference took place in 1887, and it was the Fourth Conference of 1902 that passed a resolution in favour of imperial preference. The 1902 resolution brought the whole subject of protection to the surface. Even if 'so doughty a Free Trader and so practised a controversialist as Sir Robert Giffen' could make up his mind that his opponents were 'densely stupid or wilfully perverse',[3] others found it more difficult, and those uncertainties of conviction and allegiance continued without a break until the war. Free Trade was still the governing orthodoxy by 1914, but the old labels of free trading consumers and protectionist manufacturers, of liberal traders and the conservative City, were no longer so easily applied. P. F. Clarke has shown how orthodox tariff reform formed part of the Tory conscience by 1910 when only a few years before Tories were convinced Free Traders; in 1913–14 Manchester men still 'talked of Free Trade and voted for Conservatism'.[4] Marrison has questioned the 'narrowly deterministic view of industry alignment that some historians have seen as operating in the Tariff Reform Campaign of 1903–13'.[15]

This is clearly a subject for debate. In the present context the point of importance is that Free Traders and Fair Traders, Liberals and Conservatives, radicals and reformers, all found comfort in inflated figures; they were inclined more to make use of them in political debate than to challenge them. Sir Robert Giffen and Sir George Paish were convinced Free Traders: 'The bedrock of Paish's economic faith' was the free, unfettered issue of new capital both colonial and foreign.[6] C. K. Hobson was a Free Trader, and so at the time was Keynes. The *Economist* and the *Statist* were Free Traders. In January 1914, a leading article in the *Economist* took care to point out that although Britain's government was still in the hands of the same Free Trade Cabinet, and the principles of Cobden were not yet discarded, the tariff reformers were proved wrong in their prediction of capital starvation for British industry; Britain was investing heavily abroad and British exports had boomed.[7]

For F. W. Hirst, editor of the *Economist*, British investments abroad testified to the rapidity with which Britain's wealth was growing; they were 'the superfluities and overflowings of our annual national savings'.[8] Paish's *Statist*, only two months before the war, congratulated itself on the spirit of enterprise in foreign investment over the past few years, as displayed by a Free Trade Britain where capital could be subscribed unhindered in any part of the world where it could most profitably be employed.[9]

The *Financial Review of Reviews*, to which J. A. Hobson contributed, was a Free Trader; the *Banker's Magazine* was Protectionist. To the *Banker's Magazine* – and to most true Conservatives by now – excessive foreign investment meant shortage of funds at home and lower prices for domestic securities. If only a tenth of British investment had found its way into domestic undertakings, 'we cannot wonder at the increase of unemployment and of distress among the working classes'.[10]

The *Economist*, the *Statist* and the *Banker's Magazine* were referring to the effects of foreign investment, yet foreign investment was barely discussed in the tariff reform debate before the end of the 1900s. It was then, and particularly after Lloyd George's 'Socialist' Budget in the autumn of 1909, that it reached the headlines. Free Traders appreciated the uninterrupted flow of capital abroad and the business that it brought in return, while Fair Traders feared the diversion of much needed capital from domestic industry. Free Traders exaggerated and gloried in the figures for capital exports. The export of capital, Peter Cain explains, was for Free Traders only an indication that surplus savings found placement abroad and benefited Britain by cheapening imports and boosting demand for exports.[11] For Free Traders investment overseas was good, and the figures were consequently inflated. For Fair Traders it was bad, and the figures were likewise inflated.

Alarm at the overabundant export of British investment and at all its consequences seemed (at least to Keynes) to have started from the excessively and uncharacteristically large total of foreign issues offered in London for subscription during 1908–9. Paish's figures, already appearing in the *Statist*, caught the eye as proof that a disproportionate amount of Britain's capital resources was finding its way overseas. The 1909 Budget brought even the City of London to life, so that 'not only did an almost unanimous City send a petition to Prime Minister Asquith', but the petition occasioned a meeting in the City chaired, 'most unusually', by Lord Rothschild.[12] Stock Exchange quotations were now being used for political purposes, and the *Economist*, while making the point, described the 'fearfully lugubrious' maiden speech of Lord Revelstoke (director of Barings) when the Lords threw out the Budget – how strange it was that a descendant of Sir Francis Baring should now be bewailing the fall in consols as a sort of national tragedy.[13] Conservatives and Fair Traders in the City, Rothschilds and Barings now amongst them, were terrified by a radical Budget and by the flight of capital abroad.

Lord Welby's reply, in the *Contemporary Review*, on behalf of Free Traders, used Paish's figures for the end of 1907 and quoted the observation that the large investment of British capital abroad had occurred simultaneously with a vast growth of British trade and prosperity.[14] Neither Revelstoke nor Welby had reason to question the conveniently large figure on which their own Fair Trade arguments also rested.

As the *Investors' Monthly Manual* discovered, it had been extremely difficult to write the financial history of 1909 without trespassing on debated political ground and taking sides in a party controversy with which we have no concern. 'The long and heated fight waged round the budget has imported into financial matters a party bitterness from which they are normally free. Both parties have been induced to base their arguments on more or less fallacious theories drawn from the Stock Exchange.'[15] In 1910, a leader writer in the *Economist* explained how, only two years before, the problem of the size and distribution of Britain's capital issues was of interest chiefly to a narrow circle of economists and statisticians; recent developments in politics had brought capital issues into everyday discussion and transformed them from an academic study into a party 'plank'.[16]

The contrast was clear. The *Economist*, a Free Trader, called attention to the fact that capital applications in 1909 were designed in the first place to develop the resources of the British Empire. Using identical evidence, the *Banker's Magazine*, a Fair Trader, pointed to Britain's industrial decline and to the problem of unemployment among the working classes.[17] It was a stale debate – what the Tory Prime Minister of 1903, A. J. Balfour, had described as 'an unprofitable battle of watchwords, behind which there [was] nothing deserving to be called independent reflection at all'.[18]

## RADICALS, REFORMERS AND THE FIGURES

Tariff reform was not alone in inflating the figures, although it influenced the thinking of Free Traders like Giffen, Paish and a younger Keynes.[19] An illuminating example is Edgar Crammond's progress from moderate estimates in 1907 as a Conservative Free Trader, to larger figures in 1911 as a Fair Trader, and finally to a very large total as national propagandist in 1915.[20]

Once the battle lines were drawn, both Free Traders and Fair Traders made use of the highest figures they could find against each other, but so did radicals and reformers, also in search of large and revealing numbers. C. K. Hobson's *Export of Capital*, written to supply a need during the peak years of preoccupation with investment overseas, was intended to study and demonstrate the benefit of foreign investment to the home country, not simply at the level of the capitalist but ultimately of Britain's wage earners. J. A. Hobson, once a radical Free Trader and by now an 'uncritical idealist',[21] drew heavily on Paish: he found it to be 'an immense positive advantage to have industries and home employment arising out of foreign investments'.[22] The force of Norman Angell's powerful argument (sadly so soon refuted) was that the solution to war was international finance, that 'overseas investment created hostages for peace'.[23] H. N. Brailsford used both Giffen and Paish to illustrate his arguments on 'real politics'. He too, like Hobson, was an underconsumptionist; the economic tap roots of imperialism were first the rapid accumulation of capital in a civilised country beyond its capacity to consume, followed by the search abroad for cheap and exploitable labour.[24]

Hobson, Angell and Brailsford found no need to question large estimates. Leo Chiozza Money, an unpredictable enthusiast and staunch Free Trader, liked to shock his audience with Paish's £4 billion to support his own argument for proper husbandry and the greater development of Britain's home resources.[25] Ramsay MacDonald, leader of the Labour Party, denounced foreign investment in one sentence while praising it in another; in either case he was happy, like Paish, to double the Inland Revenue's figure for income from foreign investment when it suited his argument.[26]

## INTERNATIONAL RIVALRY, WAR PROPAGANDA AND THE FIGURES

It was the war that both publicised inflated figures and then gave them time to ossify. Joseph Chamberlain's campaign for tariff reform was prompted by competition in foreign trade; his exaggerated figures for the decline of British exports, derived from an improbable investigation by British diplomats and consuls in 1898–9, were collected to parade the reality of German expansion.[27] Germany's 'unhelpful' attitude during the Boer War was not easily forgotten, and an article in the *Contemporary Review* (July 1901) drew attention to the fear that economic decay, and the passage of so many American, South African and Argentine securities from Britons to Continentals, would lead to military decline.[28]

At first, the argument was directed almost entirely at troop rivalry and competition – at the kind of fears promoted by E. E. Williams' *Made in Germany* (1896). Gradually it shifted focus to finance. It was significant, said the *Statist* in 1907, that naval rivalry and the building programme were 'lessening the attractiveness of German securities both in this country and in France'.[29] The bitterness that surrounded Lloyd George's Budget of 1909 encouraged innuendo. Sir Edgar Speyer, financial adviser to Mr Asquith (the Liberal Prime Minister), was a 'German', born and brought up in Germany, connected with Speyer & Co. of New York and Speyer-Ellison of Frankfurt; he himself had come to England only in 1887.[30]

In June 1914, Edgar Crammond read a paper to the Royal Statistical Society in which he supplied a detailed comparison of British and German wealth. It was an adventure in nationalist propaganda by which Britain's wealth was 'puffed' to the limit. The hope was that both Britons and Germans might yet be persuaded that German prosperity through trade was bound up with the growth of British investment; the true economic interests of Britain and Germany were 'reciprocal rather than antagonistic'. Sir George Paish, who took part in the discussion, agreed as a Free Trader that Crammond's figures showed that Germany and Britain could grow wealthy together, and his position was taken by another Free Trader, Lord Welby, when proposing the vote of thanks. It was then that the trouble started. Cornelius Rosenraad talked of the vast expansion of German trade and finance. J. Ellis Barker and a Mr Rosenbaum poured scorn on Crammond's statistics, 'more in the nature of guesses . . . than correct facts'. Barker thought he detected a Free Trade bias.[31]

Two months later, the outbreak of war put an end to reason and conciliation. War propaganda both reinforced existing estimates and encouraged further exaggeration. Years passed, the figures received official endorsement, and by the time that the war was over, doubts were forgotten and the figures established.

I have referred already to Lloyd George's 'Financial Statement' of 4 May 1915, when as Chancellor of the Exchequer he adopted Paish's figures outright; his intention was to signalise Britain's great resources in war and the capacity of its inhabitants for further taxation. Others followed, less optimistic perhaps but in the same wartime spirit of 'let's all pull together and strain every nerve'. H. C. Sonne used Paish's £4 billion portfolio/direct for the stock of British investment abroad, and took for granted Paish's £1 billion for the current state of British investment in the United States.[32] By 1915, Crammond had raised the capital value of Britain's *portfolio* investment to £3.9 billion; much more would be needed since Italy would want financial help, and little Belgium, once wealthy, was now a 'blackened ruin'.[33] Paish himself, after serving his time as Financial Adviser to the Chancellor of the Exchequer, presented a notably optimistic paper to the Royal Statistical Society in 1916. He re-used his £4 billion aggregate, now taken as stock, to explain how Britain's substantial income from overseas investment, and the realisation of some part of this capital abroad, had 'enabled the British people to provide the great sums of money they have spent upon the War'; losses by war would make Britons efficient, and the new wealth created would soon effect a complete recovery.[34]

The Germans followed suit. They too had felt the pressure of foreign competition before the war. Dr Helfferich, Director of the Deutsche Bank, published a book in 1913 that was described by Josiah Stamp as a 'clear and able attempt to get a close approximation to the aggregate income and capital [of Germany]'. The war made them less dispassionate. Stamp, writing in 1919, warned readers that 'ulterior motives were particularly likely to exist in German propaganda, and that too much credence can easily be given to vague estimates'. Helfferich, for all his care and accuracy, had intended to make out as strong a case as he could, and the financial power of Germany was further exaggerated in later wartime editions:

We [Germany] are no longer at the mercy of borrowed capital,

> nor is a financial blockade possible since the days of the Morocco and Tripoli and the Balkan crises . . . The results of the War have so far justified all we expected from Germany's economic and financial preparations . . . Whosoever fails to destroy us by steel and iron need not hope for salvation from the British Chancellor's 'silver bullets'.

Josiah Stamp, speaking of another such purveyor of figures, reported that Steinmann-Bucher (who represented the War Commission for German industry) had proclaimed Germany to have been rich before the war, still rich when he wrote in Easter 1916, and likely to be even richer after the war.[35] In the subsequent discussion, Sir George Paish agreed with Stamp's assessment of the real wealth of Germany, and drew attention to the flag-waving even before the war by which it was made to appear that 'Germany could do quite extraordinary things'.[36]

## CONCLUSION

We are not working with a figure that has been rationally conceived, fully debated, confirmed or denied. Paish published his estimates with the intention of adding a weapon to the Free Trade armoury. It suited both Free Traders and Fair Traders to maintain them. The declaration of war and the years of hostilities, propaganda and exaggeration, left minds exhausted (and focused, in any case, on the future rather than on a distant, almost legendary past). Four billion pounds as the figure for Britain's stock of investment overseas in August 1914 was now firmly established.

### Notes

1. For example, J. M. Keynes, 'Great Britain's Foreign Investments', *New Quarterly* (Feb. 1910), reprinted in Elizabeth Johnson (ed.), *The Collected Writings of John Maynard Keynes*, vol. XV (1971) pp. 54 ff. Keynes excused himself by explaining that Paish's estimates, although they did not 'pretend to be accurate in detail', might still 'show reliably the dimensions of the sums in question'.

2. E. Staley, *War and the Private Investor: A Study in the Relations of International Politics and International Private Investment* (Chicago, 1935) p. 523.
3. L. Price, 'Free Trade and Protection', *Economic Journal* (Sept. 1902) p. 307.
4. P. F. Clarke, 'The End of Laissez-Faire and the Politics of Cotton', *Historical Journal*, XV, 3 (1972) p. 512. He has written more fully on the subject in his *Liberals and Social Democrats* (Cambridge, 1978).
5. A. J. Marrison, 'Businessmen, Industries and Tariff Reform in Great Britain, 1903–1930'. *Business History*, XXV, 2 (July 1983) p. 169.
6. Avner Offer, 'Empire and Social Reform: British Overseas Investment and Domestic Politics', *Historical Journal*, 26, 1 (1983) p. 125.
7. 'Investing Abroad and at Home', *Economist*, 17 Jan. 1914, p. 113.
8. 'British Capital at Home and Abroad', *Economist*, 20 Nov. 1909, p. 1030.
9. *Statist*, 30 May 1914, p. 699.
10. 'Investments, Exports and Employment', *Banker's Magazine* (Nov. 1909) pp. 613–19; also, 'The Export of British Capital and the Decrease in the Value of Home Investments', ibid. (Sept. 1912) pp. 333–9.
11. P. J. Cain, 'Political Economy in Edwardian England: The Tariff-Reform Controversy', p. 48.
12. Y. Cassis, 'The Banking Community of London, 1890–1914', *Journal of Imperial and Commonwealth History*, XIII, 3 (May 1985) p. 121.
13. 'Lord Revelstoke's Speech', *Economist*, 27 Nov. 1909, p. 1083.
14. Welby, 'The Budget and British Capital', *Contemporary Review* (Jan. 1910) p. 84.
15. 'Financial History of the Year', *Investors' Monthly Manual* (Dec. 1909) p. 678.
16. 'Capital Applications in 1909', *Economist*, 1 Jan. 1910, p. 5.
17. 'Investments, Exports and Employment', *Banker's Magazine* (Nov. 1909) pp. 613–19, and 'The Export of British Capital and the Decrease in the Value of Home Investments', ibid. (Sept. 1912) pp. 333–9.
18. A. J. Balfour, *Economic Notes on Insular Free Trade* (pamphlet, Oct. 1903) p. 7.
19. In the 1920s Keynes became conscious of the danger of money flowing into colonial securities at the expense of home industry, and he was worried by anything that might encourage foreign borrowing unduly: *Report of the Committee on National Debt and Taxation* (the Colwyn Committee): *British Parliamentary Papers*, 1927, XI, pp. 521ff, and p. 712. Also his 'Foreign Investment and National Advantage', *Nation*, 9 Aug. 1924.
20. Crammond's thinking can be traced through his three articles: 'British Investments Abroad', *Quarterly Review* (July 1907); 'British Investments Abroad', *Quarterly Review* (July 1911); and 'The Economic Position of the Allied Powers', *Quarterly Review* (July 1915). He was Secretary of the Liverpool Stock Exchange.
21. Hobson's position is explained very fully, although not uncontroversially, by P. J. Cain, 'J. A. Hobson, Cobdenism and the Radical Theory of

Economic Imperialism, 1898–1914', *Economic History Review*, 2nd ser. XXXI, 4 (Nov. 1978) pp. 565–84.

22. J. A. Hobson, *An Economic Interpretation of Investment* (London, n.d., although based mainly on his articles in the *Financial Review of Reviews* published during the autumn of 1910) p. 102. His arguments drew again on Paish in his 'Investment Safeguards under Changing Conditions', *Financial Review of Reviews* (June 1914) pp. 643–54.
23. N. Angell, *The Great Illusion* (1910) p. 248.
24. H. N. Brailsford, *The War of Steel and Gold: A Study of the Armed Peace* (1914) pp. 63–88.
25. L. Chiozza Money, *The Nation's Wealth: Will it Endure?* (1914) pp. 63–88.
26. J. Ramsay MacDonald, MP, 'The 'Export of British Capital: A Labour View', *Financial Review of Reviews* (April 1909) pp. 13–19.
27. I discuss the reality of German competition in Britain's overseas trade in chapter VIII ('Latin American Imports') of my *Latin America and British Trade, 1806–1914* (1972) pp. 173–250 *passim*. The questionnaires and replies were published as *Opinions of HM Diplomatic and Consular Officers on British Trade Methods*, British Parliamentary Papers, 1899, XCVI.
28. 'Is Great Britain Living on its Capital?', *Contemporary Review* (July 1901) pp. 28, 33.
29. 'The German Loan', *Statist*, 27 April 1907, p. 846.
30. Correspondence between Mr Carlyon Bellairs, MP and Sir Edgar Speyer, *National Review* (Dec. 1909) pp. 706–8.
31. E. Crammond, 'The Economic Relations of the British and German Empires', *Journal of the Royal Statistical Society*, LXXVII (July 1914). The paper was read on 16 June and was followed by a particularly long discussion. Crammond had already published articles on Germany and international finance in the *Quarterly Review* of April and October 1910.
32. H. C. Sonne, *The City: Its Finance July 1914 to July 1915 and Future* (London, 1915) pp. 90, 144.
33. Crammond, 'The Economic Position of the Allied Powers', pp. 193–222.
34. Paish, 'War Finance', *Journal of the Royal Statistical Society*, LXXIX (May 1916) pp. 268, 299.
35. J. Stamp, 'The Wealth and Income of the Great Powers', *Journal of the Royal Statistical Society*, LXXXII (July 1919) pp. 463–70.
36. Ibid., p. 498.

# Part III
# Implications and Conclusions

# 4 Common Sense and the Numbers

We now have a revised figure for the stock of Britain's investment overseas just before the First World War. I have suggested that for portfolio investment Paish's estimate should be reduced by £1.1 billion, even allowing for those elements that are excluded from Paish's portfolio such as London issues from 1 January to 31 July 1914, British purchases on exchanges other than London, and unregistered securities everywhere. Sir Alexander Cairncross was worried by the size of the gap that already existed between the £1 billion conventionally estimated for British investment overseas in 1870 and the £3.7 billion estimated by Paish for the end of 1913.[1] The gap becomes even wider (and less convincing) if I have been right to reduce the 1870 figure to £500 million.[2]

British exports of capital before the war have been described as 'almost absurdly large', 'unique', 'amazing', and 'unthinkable'; it is the final adjective, unintentionally so, that is correct. Paul Arndt, in 1915, pointed to the many flaws in Paish's 1911 estimates, and compared them with a parallel set for new capital issues in London published periodically in the *Economist*. Nobody, said Arndt in conclusion, could any longer describe Paish's figures as 'exceedingly cautious valuations'. Arndt's own total for foreign investment, taken further than Paish's to include 1914, was only £3 billion.[3]

Paish's £3.7 billion at the end of 1913 is incompatible with my revised estimate of £500 million in 1870; it wears no better with such estimates as exist for the end of the 1920s. Kindersley's total for the stock of British capital overseas in 1929 was £3.4 billion, and slightly less for 1930.[4] His annual figures for new money invested in the 1920s were net of repayments, and to that extent they represent an improvement on Paish. Yet even when he made allowance for the acquisition by Britons of securities not transacted on domestic markets, for individual investment in private companies, firms and other property, and for the overseas activities of a number of British companies whose main assets were placed in the United Kingdom – none of which was included in Paish – Kindersley's stock total for 1930 was still only £3.7 billion.[5]

Kindersley was drawing on a combination of figures. He took

government and municipal stock from the *Stock Exchange Official Intelligence*, while his figure for 'British companies operating abroad but registered in the UK' was published in the *Economist*. In the last of four articles on British portfolio holdings abroad in 1930, the *Economist* felt that it could say 'with some assurance' that British long-term capital overseas, excluding defaulted bonds and the securities of defunct or dormant companies, did not exceed £4.25 billion in nominal value, and was probably more like £4 billion. The amount bought and sold on the London Stock Exchange (the sole, real basis of Paish's figure), together with securities of other British companies operating abroad and of those foreign and colonial companies that were known to be held largely in Britain, probably came to about £3.5 billion in 1930, and certainly to no more than £3.75 billion.[6]

It is true that the rate of Britain's investment overseas had declined sharply since the peak years before the war. New issues of overseas securities averaged £121.3 million annually in 1927–30 when they had been up to £177.4 million in 1910–13; more was now invested at home.[7] All the same, after allowing for disinvestment during the war, for investment elsewhere, and for the £1.1 billion recorded by the *Economist* as raised in the form of new issues in London for 1919–29 inclusive,[8] Kindersley's figure for 1929 is still more compatible with a reduced estimate of £2.6 billion than it is with Paish's estimate of as much as £3.7 billion for Britain's portfolio investment alone on 31 December 1913.

Naturally, the 1930s were a period of stagnation in foreign investment, even of decline. The figures in the last of Kindersley's articles show nominal holdings of quoted securities falling to £3.3 billion by 1938. Britain's steady and traditional growth was reversed in part by restrictions on foreign lending. But even without these restrictions, 'political uncertainties and the difficulties which may beset the conduct of international trade would have made substantial lending impossible'.[9]

## MICKEY MOUSE NUMBERS

Are we dealing, after all, with real numbers? Imlah found that by 1911 an extraordinary 10 per cent of Britain's national income was derived from the interest and dividends received on investment abroad.[10] Deane and Cole have calculated that the income earned on foreign property at the end of the nineteenth century was over 7 per cent on the nation's total income: it had been nothing at the beginning of the nineteenth century, and it was down to just over 1 per cent by the 1950s.[11] Yet their percentage was calculated from Imlah's table of income on property abroad, itself based on Paish's portfolio estimate for 1907. Aldcroft and Richardson, taking their figures from Feis (in practice Paish) and Imlah, accepted that foreign investment in the years before 1914 had reached 'almost 10 per cent of GNP'; income on overseas investment in the peak period 1911–13 was 'about 8½ per cent of national income'.[12] Britain's net overseas assets in 1913 were supposedly as much as a third of Britain's stock of wealth at home and abroad in 1913.[13] And what are these gigantic, manufactured numbers supposed to mean?

Weird numbers lead to odd conclusions. Capital exports by 1913, according to Brinley Thomas, accounted for 9 per cent of Britain's national income. They were 'largely portfolio rather than direct'; they were 'mainly in securities yielding a fixed return'; the 'plantation type of investment associated with the colonies' had no permanent place, and the greater part of British capital 'went to developing countries of recent settlement, particularly the overseas descendants of Western Europe – the United States, Canada, Australia and New Zealand'.[14] Thomas, like the tariff reformers, believed that Britain, by investing so much abroad, was sacrificing domestic productivity and employment; 'the pursuit of private investment profits overseas had become inconsistent with the long-run social productivity of the British economy in a changed environment'.[15] But what if this view were too pessimistic for Britain's industrial performance at home and for its competitiveness overseas? What if it were too dependent on an inflated estimate of the volume of Britain's investment abroad, or on a mistaken notion of that investment's geographical or functional distribution – or both?

The debate over whether Britain's economy fell into decline is still in progress, although it is quite some time since Peter Payne described the hypothesis of entrepreneurial failure in the late Victorian economy as having recently taken 'quite a beating'.[16] Did Britain's exports perform so badly as was thought, before 1914? We have come a long way since Ross Hoffman's pessimistic diagnosis of British trade performance against Germany, published over half a century ago.[17] The starvation of capital for domestic investment in favour of foreign investment is even now disputed. It is argued quite extensively by Matthews, Feinstein and Odling-Smee although they concede, finally, that they do not feel very convinced of the damage brought by capital shortages under any heading – markets, labour, entrepreneurship or saving.[18] The suggestion that less investment had actually reached (and remained) abroad by August 1914, and that it was differently distributed, may help to reinforce these doubts.

## RATES OF RETURN

Much the same could be true of rates of return. If investment abroad were earning 6 to 8 per cent on average holdings before the war, rather than the 5.2 per cent accepted equally by Paish and Imlah, then the annual income from as much as Paish's £3.7 billion portfolio would have had to have reached £222–296 million – far higher than Paish could himself have calculated from his amalgam of income tax returns and the revenue on unrecorded investment. Paish was compelled to deduce so high a total for capital holdings because he started, at 5.2 per cent over twenty years' purchase, with so low a level of capitalisation. This 5.2 per cent, calculated by Paish on his total for the end of *1907*, was Imlah's figure for the average return six years later (*1913*), although a steady advance of the rate of return had long and widely been experienced. Even for domestic securities at the end of 1913, British investors were recorded as not looking at 4 per cent; 'they want 5 to 6 per cent or more'.[19] British Government consols, at current prices, earned well over 3 per cent, and the return on government securities had risen all over the world.

The real rate of return, as Lance Davis and Robert Huttenback have found, is a more controversial figure than one might expect; it excites tempers since most of the imperial rhetoric has been cast in those terms.[20] Davis and Huttenback themselves have made much progress by calculating the rate of return on the adjusted book value of assets, and this is probably as far as we can get at present.

Meanwhile, one of the more active of recent controversies among economic historians has turned on the success or otherwise of the late Victorian economy, one aspect of which was the relative return on domestic and overseas investment.[21] Yet for all its technical skill, no argument can be at ease with itself that starts from a base of £4 billion as the 'stock' figure for British investment abroad (portfolio and direct) at the end of 1913, whether it comes from Imlah or from

Paish. Furthermore, Imlah had followed Paish when he had arrived at that identical 5.2 per cent as the average rate of return on Britain's overseas investment; while Paish had drawn his figure from the tax year 1907–8,[22] he himself, characteristically, had spread it over the whole period 1886–1913.[23] Then C. K. Hobson also used Paish; he accepted Paish's estimate of £140 million for earnings received in 1907 and employed it, like Imlah, to form one magnitude of a ratio, the other composed of Inland Revenue tax returns taken backwards and forwards over forty years; the results within his own time, said a contemporary critic, were 'rather astonishing'.[24]

The formula used by Paish and his successors for the rate of return was the percentage earned on capital employed. Even when Paish was first writing (in 1909) good class foreign government bonds were yielding about 5 per cent.[25] These were the safest, most respectable securities outside the British Empire, and others, less impressive, could expect to pay more. The *Economist*, in an article on 5 per cent as the 'safe' return to which most investors aspired, agreed that few British railways could offer as much, but that the preference stock of good lines abroad, especially Argentine railways, was already earning well over that amount.[26]

If, then, the yield on first-class British securities was as high as 3½ to 4 per cent in the summer of 1912,[27] if consols stood at 3.4 per cent in 1913 and the market for high-class bills was 4.37 per cent,[28] if the best of all Empire stock, that of the Canadian Government, were paying 4 per cent and the city of Montreal 4½ per cent,[29] then the average rate on *all* classes of international securities at the end of 1913 was unlikely to have remained as low as 5.2 per cent. This was indeed the case, since in 1913 the average return on the highest and most expensive classes of overseas securities in London – bonds, debentures and government and municipal loans – was already 5.1 per cent.[30] Paish, in calculating his 5.2 per cent average, was arguing from what he took to be the experience of British overseas investors in 1907–8. R. A. Lehfeldt calculated that the rate on foreign *fixed-interest* bonds in 1913 was by now 5.45 per cent, while on other *fixed-interest* foreign investment it was 5.79 per cent.[31] A table of dividends for the main British investment trusts (percentage on par of *common* stock) showed that in 1913 the return varied from 7 to 14 per cent over the seven companies surveyed.[32]

Two puzzles remain – first, the numbers themselves and their implications for the shape of the British economy, and then the distribution of investments once the figures have been revised and brought up to date. I come now, in the two chapters that follow, to my suggestions for a rather different pattern of geographical and occupational distribution among Britain's overseas investment as it existed in 1914.

## Notes

1. A. K. Cairncross, *Home and Foreign Investment, 1870–1913: Studies in Capital Accumulation* (Cambridge, 1953) p. 186.
2. D. C. M. Platt, 'British Portfolio Investment Overseas before 1870: Some Doubts', *Economic History Review*, 2s. XXXII, 1 (Feb. 1980) p. 13.
3. P. Arndt, 'Neue Beiträge zur Frage der Kapitalanlage im Ausland', *Zeitschrift für Socialwissenschaft*, N.F., VI (1915), article no. 3 ('Zur Statistik der Kapitalanlagen im Ausland').
4. Robert Kindersley, 'British Foreign Investments in 1930', *Economic Journal* (June 1932) p. 190.
5. Ibid., pp. 193, 198.
6. 'British Capital Abroad', *Economist*, 25 Oct. 1930, p. 751. The other three articles in this useful series are to be found in the *Economist* for 1 March (p. 453); 22 March (pp. 634–5); and 18 Oct. (pp. 699–700), all in 1930.
7. A. T. K. Grant, *A Study of the Capital Market in Britain from 1919–1936* (1967 edn) p. 170. His figures came from those published by the Midland Bank.
8. Compiled by John Atkin, 'Official Regulation of British Overseas Investment, 1914–1931', *Economic History Review*, 2s. XXIII, 2 (1970) Appendix Table 1, p. 335.
9. Sir Robert Kindersley, 'British Overseas Investments, 1938', *Economic Journal* (Dec. 1939) pp. 692, 695.
10. Albert Imlah, *Economic Elements in the Pax Britannica* (Cambridge, Mass., 1958) pp. 73–5.
11. P. Deane and W. A. Cole, *British Economic Growth, 1688–1959* (Cambridge, 1964) p. 293.
12. Derek H. Aldcroft and Harry W. Richardson, *The British Economy 1870–1939* (1969) pp. 64, 84–5.
13. The figure comes from Michael Edelstein, 'Foreign Investment and Empire, 1860–1914', in Roderick Floud and Donald McCloskey (eds), *The Economic History of Britain since 1700*, vol. II (Cambridge, 1981) p. 70.
14. B. Thomas, 'The Historical Record of International Capital Movements to 1913', in John H. Adler (ed.), *Capital Movements in Economic Development* (New York, 1967) p. 15.

15. Ibid., p. 31.
16. In Peter Mathias and M. M. Postan (eds), *Cambridge Economic History of Europe*, VII, 1 (Cambridge, 1978) p. 209.
17. R. Hoffman, *Great Britain and the German Trade Rivalry, 1875–1914* (Philadelphia, 1933). Stephen Nicholas gives a more realistic picture of foreign competition in his article: 'The Overseas Marketing Performance of British Industry, 1870–1914', *Economic History Review*, 2s. XXXVII, 4 (Nov. 1984) pp. 489–506.
18. R. C. O. Matthews, C. H. Feinstein and J. C. Odling-Smee, *British Economic Growth, 1856–1970* (Oxford, 1982) pp. 353–9. Recent arguments and bibliography are brought together in Sidney Pollard's useful paper 'Capital Exports, 1870–1914: Harmful or Beneficial', *Economic History Review*, XXXVIII, 4 (1985).
19. 'The Prospect for 1914', *Investor's Review*, 27 December 1913, p. 864.
20. Lance Davis and Robert Huttenback, chapter III of a typescript now with a publisher, 'British Business and the Profits of Empire', p. 58.
21. More particularly in Donald N. McCloskey, 'Did Victorian Britain Fail?', *Economic History Review*, 2s. XXXII, 4 (1979); N. F. R. Crafts, 'Victorian Britain Did Fail', ibid., XXXII, 4 (1979); McCloskey, 'No It Did Not: A Reply to Crafts', ibid. The debate incorporates W. P. Kennedy's 'Foreign Investment, Trade and Growth in the UK, 1870–1913', *Explorations in Economic History*, 11, 4 (Summer 1974).
22. Paish (1909), p. 474.
23. A. H. Imlah, 'British Balance of Payments and the Export of Capital, 1816–1913', *Economic History Review*, 2s. V, 2 (1952) pp. 223, 238–9; and ibid., *Economic Elements in the Pax Britannica*, p. 180.
24. Review of Hobson's *Export of Capital* in the *Journal of the Royal Statistical Society*, 78 (Jan. 1915) p. 96.
25. *Economist*, 30 Jan. 1909, p. 216.
26. 'A Review of Five Per Cent Securities', *Economist*, 6 Feb. 1909, p. 265.
27. 'The Depreciation of Gilt-Edged Securities', *Investors' Monthly Manual* (July 1912) p. 411.
28. David K. Sheppard, *The Growth and Role of UK Financial Institutions, 1880–1962* (1971) p. 190.
29. *Investor's Monthly Manual* (April 1913), p. 174.
30. 'The Capital Market', *Economist*, Commercial History and Review of 1913, 21 Feb. 1914, p. 418.
31. R. A. Lehfeldt, 'The Rate of Interest on British and Foreign Investments', *Journal of the Royal Statistical Society*, LXXVII, IV (March 1914) pp. 432, 435.
32. A. Emil Davies, *Investments Abroad* (Chicago, 1927) p. 161.

# 5 Second Thoughts on the Geographical Distribution of British Investment

## THE EXISTING FIGURES

Conventional wisdom for the geographical spread of British investment just before the First World War, even today, is derived directly from Sir George Paish's figures as published in the *Statist* of February 1914. Once challenged, the inescapable 'supplementary' is the difference to be expected after a general reduction of Paish's estimates when applied, more specifically, to the distribution of British overseas investment by country, area or region in August 1914; Chapter 6 will say something about the same problem as applied to functions.

With the important exception of the United States, Paish found that Britain's greatest investments were in the 'daughter States of the Empire' and in Britain's 'great Indian possessions'; British investment elsewhere was 'largely confined to the young countries of America', of which Argentina took the major part.[1] Paish's distribution was as set out in Table 5.1.

Subsequently, Paish's figures have resurfaced quite frequently. Feis's total for 'Long-term Publicly Issued British Capital Investment in Other Lands', December 1913, is Paish as altered significantly only for Russia.[2] Sir Alec Cairncross employed a mixture of Paish (1911) and Paish (1914), to which he added a larger amount for India.[3] J. H. Lenfant used Paish both for the geographical and for the functional distribution of British investment in 1913.[4] A. R. Hall reproduced the figures from Feis.[5] Michael Edelstein uses Paish (via Feis) for the stock of British investments in the United States in 1914.[6] Standard textbooks echo the standard view, and a recent version draws on Paish (as reproduced in Feis) for the notion that 'the flow of British capital exports was increasingly directed towards America and the Empire, between 1870 and 1914'.[7]

The warnings of contemporaries have not been observed. Paish

Table 5.1 Paish's geographical distribution of Britain's portfolio investment abroad, 31 December 1913 (major countries, £ millions rounded to nearest £100 000)

| | | |
|---|---|---|
| *British Empire* | | |
| Australia | 332.1 | |
| Canada and Newfoundland | 514.9 | |
| India and Ceylon | 378.8 | |
| New Zealand | 84.3 | |
| South Africa | 370.2 | |
| Others | 99.7 | |
| Total | | £1780.0 |
| *Foreign Countries* | | |
| Argentina | 319.6 | |
| Brazil | 148.0 | |
| Chile | 61.1 | |
| China | 43.9 | |
| Egypt | 45.0 | |
| Japan | 62.6 | |
| Mexico | 99.0 | |
| Russia | 66.6 | |
| United States | 754.6 | |
| Others | 334.1 | |
| Total | | £1934.7 |
| TOTAL (British and Foreign) | | £3714.7 |

*Source*: Paish (1914) p. vi.

constructed a total of annual issues – an accumulation of 'flows'. As A. W. Flux pointed out at the discussion of Paish's first paper, presumably himself with a stock figure in mind, investments had shifted (within Europe particularly) so that the securities that had been held by Britons in great quantities were now (1909) 'largely held by neighbouring countries'.[8] The *Economist*, looking more broadly at the way in which contemporary estimates were influenced by the political importance now attached to capital exports, found that although the final totals for investment generally may not have differed very widely, *within* those totals there was a 'striking divergency in the allocation of investment to the various parts of the world'.[9]

If, as in Paish, the totals for investment allocated to each country are taken as the sum of fifty to sixty years, they are unlikely to bear a close resemblance to the preferences of investors for the last six years, 1908–13. Paish's breakdown by country, 1908 to 1913, was published in his paper of February 1914. A matching set, slightly superior in quality but taken from the same material, was supplied annually by the *Investor's Monthly Manual*. It gave the following results (Table 5.2):

*Table* 5.2 Geographical distribution of new issues in London, 1908–13 (major countries, £ millions rounded to nearest £100 000)

| | *1908* | *1909* | *1910* | *1911* | *1912* | *1913* | *TOTAL* |
|---|---|---|---|---|---|---|---|
| *British Empire* | | | | | | | |
| Australasia | 4.0 | 11.4 | 13.4 | 3.3 | 13.5 | 18.6 | 64.2 |
| Canada | 27.8 | 26.8 | 36.9 | 41.2 | 47.0 | 44.1 | 223.8 |
| India and Ceylon | 13.1 | 15.3 | 18.0 | 5.2 | 3.7 | 3.8 | 59.1 |
| South Africa | 6.2 | 11.3 | 3.4 | 4.4 | 3.9 | 6.3 | 35.5 |
| Others | 7.4 | 9.9 | 20.7 | 10.9 | 4.6 | 3.3 | 56.8 |
| *Foreign Countries* | | | | | | | |
| Argentina | 15.0 | 21.7 | 22.9 | 16.7 | 20.1 | 12.0 | 108.4 |
| Brazil | 13.0 | 9.2 | 11.8 | 19.2 | 14.4 | 15.1 | 82.7 |
| Chile | 1.3 | 4.1 | 4.7 | 8.3 | 1.0 | 0.4 | 19.8 |
| China | 5.0 | 0.7 | 1.6 | 7.4 | 6.0 | 6.9 | 27.6 |
| Japan | 2.9 | 4.7 | nil | nil | 3.2 | nil | 10.8 |
| Mexico | 8.1 | 9.1 | 5.1 | 2.6 | 4.1 | 10.6 | 39.6 |
| Russia | 3.8 | 9.5 | 4.0 | 5.2 | 10.5 | 9.0 | 42.0 |
| United States | 21.5 | 15.9 | 39.6 | 21.3 | 23.6 | 18.7 | 140.6 |
| Others | 12.9 | 14.0 | 25.1 | 19.9 | 10.0 | 11.7 | 93.6 |

*Source*: *Investor's Monthly Manual* (December issues).

Paish's figures for December 1913 (Table 5.1) place the United States far ahead of any other destination for Britain's portfolio investment, at £754.6 million, to Canada's £514.9 million, Australasia's £416.4, India and Ceylon at £378.8 and South Africa at £370.2. These were estimates of investment supplied over the previous fifty to sixty years. Yet for 'new issues' in the years 1908 to 1913 Canada was well to the front with £223.8 million, with the United States at only £140.6, and India/Ceylon and South Africa now far below Argentina, Brazil and even Australasia. This was no six-year wonder; the pattern of investment had changed not only for new issues but also for former issues bought and resold on the secondary market.

## BRITISH INVESTORS AND FOREIGN SECURITIES

The United States was a major focus for British investment before 1914. It was prosperous, politically stable, and, with notorious exceptions, reliable. The United States was the first of the regions of large-scale European settlement, and the most successful.

However, the confirmed and massive lead of the United States in Paish's 'flow' statistics over fifty to sixty years is an unreliable guide to its relative position in British overseas investment by August 1914. Britons in 1914 had more money invested in the United States than in any other foreign nation. But they are unlikely to have had more than *twice* as much as they had in their new favourite, Argentina. Nor was the United States, any longer, the destination of 'over a third of the whole British investment outside the empire',[10] or of not less than one-fifth of Britain's total investment overseas.[11] Argentina first entered Britains's financial markets, on a significant scale, only in the second half of the 1880s; it then vanished for a decade after the Baring collapse of 1890–91. But in and after 1904 Argentina, with Canada, became the darlings of the British investor.

The one, overwhelmingly familiar feature of British investment in the United States – by no means exclusively a post-war phenomenon or the 'result of war-time liquidations'[12] – was the declining importance of US securities in British portfolios from as early as the *1890s*. There are many peculiarities in the investment policy of a marine insurance company, but B. L. Anderson's investigation of the composition of the Union Marine Insurance Company's portfolio for 1897 to 1915 has shown the disposal of almost two-thirds of its US holdings.[13] Among all Scottish trust companies, as W. Turrentine Jackson confirms, there was a policy of reducing the proportion of US securities in their funds during those years before the war that coincided with a steady shift from railways to 'industrials'; money was channelled to South America or to the Empire, and although Scots still had investments rather larger in the United States by 1914 than they had had at the low point of 1900 (after the depression of the 1890s), their US securities now formed a smaller percentage of total Scottish capital invested abroad.[14]

For Scotland, the peculiar strength of Edinburgh and Glasgow finance meant that the disposal of US securities by traditional business was compensated for by an increase in mortgages and in the stake of investment companies. This was not so obviously the case further south, nor was it within the discretion of Britons themselves. The United States had much less need by now for capital imports. Lance Davis explains that, with the exception of the Southern States, the US economy 'moved gradually towards a national capital market in the period 1870–1914';[15] shortly before the war, US capital markets for domestic securities 'were probably as good as the English'.[16] The US Government had long since discontinued large-scale borrowing in London. Railway bond issues were still floated on British and Continental markets. But there was money enough locally to cope with most 'industrials', and very little sale in London (1913) for American State and municipal bonds other than those of New York City.[17]

Whatever the case, and the reduction in overseas borrowing is not in doubt, the United States was and remained the 'single most important foreign source of new security issues in the British capital market'.[18] Admittedly, the London market was central to the disposal of US securities throughout Europe, so that the numbers tend to mislead if taken for 'British' participation alone. But it is a matter of scale; the United States was still borrowing more from abroad than anyone else, although proportionately less so than it had during the peak of the 1870s and 1880s. Paish believed in the continued and massive survival of US railway securities in British ownership after the early 1890s, and they formed more than 80 per cent of his total for portfolio investment in the United States at the end of 1913. I shall return to Britain's interest in US 'rails' when discussing the distribution of British investment by function in the next chapter. Meanwhile, I find it difficult to reconcile the £282 million of Kindersley's more comprehensive estimate for British investment outstanding in the United States in 1935, war losses notwithstanding,[19] with Paish's £755 million for portfolio investment alone at the end of 1913.

British investment in the United States was by far the largest figure, foreign or Empire, on Paish's list. Other cases exist where Paish's geographical distribution suggests peculiar conclusions. For Russia it is evident that the Paish estimate for 'British' portfolio investment of £66.6 million at the end of 1913, and even more so Feis's revised figure of £110 million, incorporated heavy investment by France (via London) in Russian securities, especially government and municipal loans.

Much the same was true of 'British' investment in such countries as Mexico and Brazil.[20] Both republics were large importers of capital in the years leading up to the war, and Brazil, by the first half of 1911, was actually second among foreign states applying to the London Stock Exchange. *The Times*, in 1908, had described London's portion of a large issue by the State of São Paulo as an 'exceptionally well-secured investment' in its class.[21] Yet Dutchmen in particular were keen on Brazilian loans, wherever issued, and the difficulty is to isolate Britain's own contribution. Continental purchasing through London of Brazilian issues was known to be 'conspicuously high' before the war.[22] The problem with Paish, by whom Brazil was credited with no less than £148 million of British portfolio investment in December 1913, is that his number was distorted by Brazil's rubber boom and by the current price of coffee. Both, unfortunately, were transient and exceptional. Brazil's wild rubber could not compete with the product of the new plantations in Ceylon and Malaya. Brazilian coffee, sold at 14 cents early in 1913, fetched $5\frac{3}{4}$ cents after only a year. Underwriters of Brazil's £11 million loan of May 1913, even as issued by Rothschilds, were left with 95 per cent, much of which was still on their hands six months later;[23] the price, in fact, dropped nearly three points below the level at which it had been offered to the public.[24] The boom in foreign investment in Brazil was over and applications for new capital in London in 1914 were down to a third of Argentina's.

Likewise, Paish's figure for Mexico must have been too high. Mexico, incredibly, brought out an important loan in London in 1913 without help from the underwriters.[25] But it was experiencing a rare lull in its 'Revolution', and it was shortly at war again; Mexican securities, like Brazil's, had slumped on the London Market by January 1914.[26] Mexico stands at £99 million on Paish's list, when even a journalist's 'puff' in the *Financial Review of Reviews*, March 1913, put British investment no higher than £64 million.[27] With such extraordinary figures, it is difficult enough to believe that British holdings in Latin America could have been as high as Paish said for 1913, and even more difficult to accept the £1.2 billion estimated by Irving Stone.[28]

The only substantial change to be made by Herbert Feis to Paish's geographical distribution, as I have said, was to increase British investment in Russia.[29] Although quoted confidently by Falkus,[30]

Feis's number must be mistaken. It is true that British lending to Russia increased remarkably in the years immediately before the war, in 'municipals', trade, manufacturing and oil. Russian new issues in London, in 1914, amounted to £12.7 million, higher than for either 1912 or 1913. But there was much ground to be made up. Britain's longstanding dislike of Russian securities was well understood. Paish's total includes an unrealistic amount for Russian Government stock, in which too much credit is given to British subscribers in the disposal of such gigantic loans as those of 1906 and 1909. Feis, in up-valuing Paish, seems to have taken London's portion (£13 million) of the loan of 1906 as subscribed by Britons, when we know that the major part was bought for the Continent.[31] Much the same was true of a similarly large government loan in 1909, mentioned earlier.

The Continent had long been interested in Russian Government issues – the Dutch always, the Germans from the late sixties, and the French after the late eighties. Holland, in the mid-1900s, was described as having 'poured money into shares in Russian oil companies'.[32] But investors in Britain, even in the mid-1900s, had nothing to do with Russian bonds,[33] and besides, although France had become an immensely important market for Russian securities in general, a very considerable drift of securities back to Russia was already taking place (together with large, initial sales to Russia's own domestic investors both at St Petersburg and on Western European exchanges). Yves Guyot, editor of the *Journal des Economistes*, quoted the belief of a Mr A. Raffalovich, agent in Paris for the Russian Ministry of Finance, that the share of Russian capitalists in the ownership of their national debt shortly before the war was nearly half of the entire amount.[34] In private funding, Hain Barkai, although he acknowledges the importance of foreign entrepreneurship, is right in his claim that pre-war Russia financed its industrialisation almost entirely from its domestic resources.[35]

The numbers are less dramatic for the Far East, and the problem for China (although far less so for Japan) is much complicated by the great volume of European, 'direct' investment through such foreign business centres as Hong Kong and Shanghai. But on Paish's estimates for China and Japan, £43.9 million and £62.8 million respectively, it should be said that not only were Chinese securities particularly well known to have been bought through London for sale on the Continent, but so indeed were the issues of the government of Japan. We have seen what happened to national 'tranches' of the Japanese War Loans in the mid-1900s. Harold G. Moulton calculated Japan's total foreign indebtedness at 2.1 billion yen (£214 million) in the year ending 31 December 1913, of which about 1.5 billion yen took the form of National Government issues outstanding abroad.[36] It seems unlikely that as much as 30 per cent, dominated as it was by 1.2 billion yen of National Government securities from the Russo–Japanese War, was in British hands by the end of 1913. In fact, although Japan preferred to issue its loans in sterling until as late as 1910, government applications thereafter were denominated, more realistically, in francs.

Misattributions on this scale are worth pursuing. The Royal Institute of International Affairs chose to generalise from Feis, and hence from Paish. Feis and Paish estimated large amounts for British investment in the United States, Brazil, Mexico and Russia. Yet even Pais and Feis would have been surprised by the institute's ingenuous deduction that since industrialisation in the United States 'had proceeded only a little way' by 1913, and since Russian industry was 'still untouched', it was probably right to say that less than 3 per cent of Britain's overseas investments just before the war found a home in countries not essentially producers of primary products; more than 80 per cent went to countries largely dependent on the export of primary produce.[37]

## BRITISH INVESTORS AND EMPIRE SECURITIES

Paish saw the United States and the British Empire (of which the 'great Indian possessions' were the major component) as the focus of British investment overseas. Taken over half a century, he was right. But such a distribution is no longer so obvious for the preferences of British investors during the investment boom in and after 1908.

It is not improbable that more recent approaches have been influenced overmuch by attitudes to investment in the Empire that circulated after the First World War. Furthermore, it must be said that speakers on both sides of the tariff reform debate (including Paish himself) came to attach disproportionate importance to Empire trade and investment even *before* 1914. Shortly before the war, when Australia resurfaced as a borrower, Britons were to show a preference for Empire investment, particularly in the 'white' Dominions. Among the new capital issues of the first half of 1914, the *Economist* found that the requirements of Canada and Australia had placed British Empire lending ahead of the figure for foreign countries – 'an occurrence which is quite unusual'.[38]

It was not until the inter-war years that British investors came under pressure to give preference to Empire securities. Preferential trade within the Empire had been accepted by Britain since 1919, and preference spread more gradually to the regulation of investment overseas, to the extent that in the Defence regulations of 1937 all capital issues were forbidden without Treasury agreement.[39] The pressures were simply political; greater incentives both for investment and trade were to be found elsewhere. Two-thirds of Britain's emigrants in the 1920s went to Canada, Australia and New Zealand; the financing of development meant that Empire public bodies and companies borrowed £705 million in London between 1920 and 1929. Much extra investment took the form of the London issues and retained earnings of British companies operating wholly or partly overseas – 'mines, oil companies, tea, coffee, and rubber plantations'.[40] The report of the 'Macmillan' Committee, the Committee on Finance and Industry, made a point early in the Slump of urging British investors to put their money into British-owned enterprises abroad (principally, although not entirely, in the Colonies); this was preferable to the misdirection of British energy and capital into foreign government and municipal loans 'which absorb our available foreign balance while doing little for our industry and commerce'.[41]

Before the war, the benefits of investing outside the Empire were sufficient to overcome whatever slight advantage might exist for the British Dominions and colonies, and British Government pressures even after the war were not always effective. Quite independently of those Colonial Trustee Acts that encouraged the growth, 'not always prudent', of Dominion borrowing in London, both trade and finance increasingly followed the flag. Kindersley supposed that from the end of 1930 the defaults in Latin America and the German moratorium must have had something to do with the decline of interest in foreign securities,[42] and he was surely right. But the trend towards Empire trade and investment that characterised the inter-war years, although strong at the time, had been scarcely discernible before 1914. Australia, India and South Africa took a considerable share of the investment recorded in Paish's aggregate figures, and thereby reflect much genuine interest before 1900. They became important again in the inter-war years. They were less significant within the preferences of British investors during the boom years before August 1914.

Australia was not interested in foreign investment until 1909, and even then it did not start borrowing again on an ample scale until 1912. The great era for British investment in Australia had been between 1875 and 1891. Over the whole period since the foundation of the colony to the end of 1913, the total amount actually raised by the Australian authorities, including State financing of railways and utilities, is calculated at £391.8 million.[43] Australia's banking crisis of 1893, overstocking in the pastoral industry and a catastrophic drought in 1901–2, meant that the level of real income per capita reached in 1890 was not regained until 1907.[44] While customarily a borrower overseas, Australia, more particularly from 1904 to 1911, became a net lender.[45] The Dominions Royal Commissioners, taking evidence in April 1913 from Robert Lucas Nash, now editor of the *Sydney Telegraph* and for long a London financial journalist of good repute, were interested, if not wholly convinced, by his 'remarkable' conclusions in which, amongst other things, he declared that Australia as a whole now owed less overseas than it had ten years before.[46] For both Australia and New Zealand, partly because they wanted it themselves, money was raised at home. Sir George Dibbs, Premier of New South Wales, was not unrepresentative in his wish that perhaps within twelve months (of 1893) and certainly within two years, he could see his way 'never to borrow another shilling on the English market'.[47]

Dibbs had his timing wrong; he was speaking just before the great bank crash. But his expectations were realistic. The capacity of the Dominions to finance themselves was demonstrably the case well before the war. Australia and New Zealand never again felt the need for the extravagant capital imports of the 1870s and 1880s. Before the London market reopened to international issues in 1904, New Zealand had become accustomed to draw both on its domestic investors and on neighbouring Australians.[48] Australian State governments, like New South Wales and Victoria, were able to borrow locally at or near 3½ per cent for a full twenty years before the First World War.[49]

The process started earlier for Australia than elsewhere; over 30 per cent of the public debt was raised at home by 1914.[50] But even for Argentina, Britain's 'honorary' Dominion, where 85 per cent of the national funded debt was estimated as being held abroad in 1914, only about half was still foreign-owned by 1930, so that 'most of the net increase in the debt from 1914 to 1930 came from domestic sources'.[51] In Canada, large-scale borrowing overseas did not begin until 1905, by which time accelerated economic expansion had already been experienced for a decade.[52] Ian Drummond reminds us that local finance and local financial institutions were of great importance to colonial businesses and governments – 'of far greater importance than the existing literature suggests'.[53]

In some respects this was less true for India, although it was fast coming to be the case. By 1930, the *Economist* commented on the comparatively low proportion of British ownership in companies registered both in the Dominions *and* in India; it appeared that the majority of their share capital had been raised on the spot.[54] Keynes had sensed this as early as 1909, when he explained that most of the £48 million he calculated as invested in joint-stock companies registered in India, in municipal debentures and in port trusts, was held in India.[55] What is 'surprising and certainly most gratifying', said the *Economist* in 1911, 'is to discover the extent to which [industrial development] is being financed by India itself'. While the government and local authorities borrowed money in Britain to pay for all large undertakings, the commercial community of India was meeting its own needs with comparatively little help from abroad. Indians, the editorialist said, dominated the ownership of the textile mills; they accounted for 50 per cent of the tea plantations and nearly 20 per cent of India's coal mines.[56] Chandavarkar has concluded very recently that the 'bulk of internal trade and economic activity' was financed by the unorganised, domestic money market right through from the Mutiny to the end of British India in 1947.[57]

Nor is it any longer so reasonable to assume that those large official borrowings, for Indian railways and governments, were predominantly made and held abroad. Government securities were widely owned in India itself, and after the abandonment of the railway guarantee system in 1870 British investors were not easily attracted to Indian railway stocks – 'the average rate of return (on Indian railways) in the early twentieth century was never more than 3¾ per cent, while Latin American and North American railway stocks were paying between 4 and 5 per cent'.[58] Indian Government securities were notoriously stagnant in London in the decade before 1914, with only the occasional and surprising exception like the Loans of May 1907 and January 1908. A very large 3½ per cent Rupee Loan issued in London just under par, for the equivalent of £30 million, was reported by the *Economist* as 'almost entirely subscribed in India'.[59] It was a low-priced investment, and it was taken within India itself as early as 1897.

Precise figures for British investment in India before the First World War have been the subject of much debate, not always 'scientific'. One example among many was the angry exchange published in the *Economic Journal* of 1932–3, when estimates of British capital in India just before the Slump ranged between the 'quite astronomical' £1 billion of G. D. Birla, and V. K. R. V. Rao's £575 million, the ('at most') £500 million of G. F. Shirras, and the *Economist*'s £354 million.[60] Much needs to be unscrambled. But it would seem unlikely that 'some 70 per cent to 75 per cent' of recorded investment in India (unless the definition of 'recorded' is much restricted) had come from abroad by the beginning of the First World War.[61]

The Paish estimate of British portfolio investment in South Africa, in December 1913, reached £370 million. The problem is not the domestic contribution by contrast with foreign, as it was for Australia and India; it is rather the proportion of foreign investment that should properly be assigned to Britons. S. Herbert Frankel seems to have accepted Paish's understanding that the proportion of South African mining shares held on the Continent was 'inconsiderable in comparison with the quantity held in Great Britain'.[62] Frankel acknowledges that there was evidence both of substantial German entrepreneurial activity in individual gold mines and of German and French ownership of South African mining shares, but he agreed with Paish that 8 per cent was a sufficient allowance for the Continental share of new capital subscribed for South Africa.[63] The clue is here, since it was what happened to the shares *after* issue in London that mattered; loans in London were bought by Continentals at the time of issue and even more so once they entered the 'secondary market'. It is unfortunate, too, that Frankel has made the usual mistake of treating Paish's accumulated figure for South Africa as if it were a stock estimate for the end of 1913.[64]

The discovery of diamonds (1867–70) marked the beginning of South Africa's 'mineral revolution', and from the 1880s gold outmatched diamonds; by 1912 'over a quarter of the national product was derived from mining'.[65] The 'Kaffir Boom' of 1895 (in the securities of South African gold mines) was truly international 'in the sense that dealings in the same shares of mining companies in the Transvaal took place simultaneously in London, Paris, Berlin, Brussels and Johannesburg'.[66]

The enthusiasm of French speculators lasted only nine months, and vanished in the autumn of 1895. Britons were dismayed by the failure of the Jameson Raid at the end of 1895 and by the news of the Kaiser's telegram; they turned their attention to 'Westralians' (gold mines in Western Australia). The price of South African mining securities in London collapsed, from a peak of $19\frac{5}{8}$ for Consolidated Goldfields in 1895 to only $3\frac{3}{4}$ in 1897. Political unease continued right up to the declaration of war in October 1899 after which peace was not concluded until May 1902. Both British investors and French were by now out of South African gold mines and only Germans remained, so much so that 'a small army of travelling salesmen' is described as selling 'Kaffirs' throughout Germany in the 1900s.[67]

If 'new' issues are not to be taken as the single criterion (as they were by both Paish and Frankel), there is much to be said for Robert Kubicek's view that although South African mining companies might have been registered in (or managed from) Johannesburg and London, their capital by the mid-1900s was mainly retained on the Continent, 'a pattern which held until the outbreak of World War I'.[68] The 'Kaffir Circus' in London was described by the *Economist* in 1906 as dragging out its dismal days,[69] and Kubicek quotes the opinion of a senior partner in Wernher Beit for 1913 to the effect that South African mines were a 'dead letter' in London and 'nobody wants to touch them'.[70] Generally speaking, South African *Government* securities were also unpopular in London in the 1900s. Canada took what money was available, and it was only when Canada overstepped the mark that South African Government stock was to be seen once more. Even then, two South African Government loans of 1914 were left 65 and 80 per cent respectively with the underwriters.

Within Paish's estimate for South Africa, more than a third consisted of the capital of mining companies.[71] Much the same ratio was given by the *Economist* in its breakdown of South African investment for June 1911 (£71.5 million in Transvaal gold mines and £12.6 million in individual mines, out of a total paid-up capital of £256.6 million).[72] The amount is large, and consequently the nationality of ownership important. As for public authorities, the *Stock Exchange Official Intelligence* gave £134.7 million as the total actually raised from its beginning in the nineteenth century, until the end of 1913,[73] of which, by then, much must have been authorised or taken up by domestic investors. If the high proportion of Kaffirs held on the Continent, amortisation and the homeward drift of public securities are all taken into account, then £370 million (Paish's total for South Africa) no longer makes sense for 'stock' at the end of 1913.

## BRITISH INVESTORS AND REGIONS OF RECENT SETTLEMENT

Paish's geographical distribution is obviously inaccurate for 'stock', however true it may have been for 'flows'. I doubt whether Paish, at least when he began, ever expected it to be such. He was an experienced journalist, co-editor of a leading financial weekly in the world's most important money market. He must have been well aware of current trends. No doubt the magic of numbers and the pressure of contemporary public opinion helped to persuade him to claim more than he had actually established; Paish's achievement in opening up the subject and confirming 'flows' was surely enough. Later generations have many advantages over him, and from where we ourselves stand it is easier to see the extent to which the geographical distribution of Britain's stock of investments overseas, by August 1914, had shifted. Britons, traditionally, preferred the Empire and the United States. They now, quite understandably, took an interest in a new generation of seekers after capital that promised bilateral trade, political security, and ample opportunities for sustained growth – that is, temperate regions of recent European settlement.

I am talking about areas of abnormal immigration between the 1870s and 1914. The United States was already established and self-sustaining. Australia, although expanding very rapidly in the later decades of the nineteenth century, virtually disappeared from international capital markets after the banking crisis of 1893. South Africa was never in the same class. Ragnar Nurkse ranges too widely when he identifies as regions of recent settlement a huge category that includes the United States, the 'white' Dominions (Canada, South Africa and Australasia), Argentina, Uruguay and southern Brazil, to which he might well have added Chile and parts of British East Africa; it was to Canada and Argentina that attention turned in the decade before August 1914. But he is right in his general proposition that

> the main flow of capital in the nineteenth century was not to the neediest countries with their 'teeming millions', which were indeed neglected, but to sparsely peopled areas where conditions for rapid growth along familiar Western lines were exceptionally favourable.[74]

Kennedy explains how the bias in British capital markets before the war was not towards foreign investment as such but to 'safe, well-known securities in general, many of which were foreign'; it was against smaller, more profitable but riskier investment at home or abroad.[75] The investor in search of as high a rate of return as was compatible with safety was advised by the *Financial Times* in 1913 to find it in the fixed-interest-bearing securities of American, Canadian and Argentine railways, and in Canadian and South American 'municipals' and 'industrials'.[76] The Empire was a 'safe haven for British investment in the interwar years', much more so than it had been before 1914.[77]

I have written elsewhere about the remarkable attractions of both Canada and Argentina to the British investor in the decades leading up to the First World War.[78] Argentina had reached the peak of its performance, its Golden Age, and it remained immensely prosperous until 1929. Argentina was a Latin country and therefore suspect among British investors; South America was the 'land of revolutions'. But the answer to this, said the former financial editor of the *Buenos Aires Standard*, was that revolutions in the republic were as dead as the Dodo; Argentina was now ruled by agriculture and commerce, and neither would tolerate a political interruption to its 'peaceful sway'.[79] Argentina's inhabitants were Europeans, more than half immigrants or sons of immigrants; the Indian population was minute, and blacks almost non-existent.[80] Its population was rising more rapidly than Canada's, at 3.8 per cent annually from 1895 to 1914 compared with Canada's 2.3 per cent (from 1891),[81] and it had nearly twice the numbers of Australia in 1913, having grown at more than double the rate.[82] Service on Argentina's Public Debt was resumed in 1897, the exchange rate was stabilised in 1899 and the gold standard restored.

Argentina had immense natural advantages. It was the cheapest producer of wheat in the world. The cost of wheat production in Argentina, said the *Financial News* in 1894, was so low that it would 'blanch the hair of American farmers'.[83] From the turn of the century Argentine producers enjoyed a handsome monopoly of

Britain's beef imports. Chilled beef remained fresh only for forty days, and the sea passage from the River Plate to London was twenty-one to twenty-five days. Australian beef, on the longer passage, could not compete; it could do so only from the 1930s when a method for transporting quality beef over long distances was perfected. Export prices improved from the 1890s, and the terms of trade turned markedly in favour of primary producers. By 1911, Argentina's foreign trade per capita was 'almost six times the average in the rest of Latin America', and it was larger than Canada's.[84] The pampa of Argentina was much larger than the prairies of Canada, and more fully settled. There were 13 million hectares of grain under cultivation on the pampa shortly before the war and 6.7 million of alfalfa; the population was 3.2 million. By comparison, Canada's prairies had 9.2 million hectares and a rural population of 1.3 million.[85]

Anybody who writes of pre-war Argentina employs a succession of superlatives, and if Argentina appears as second to Canada with British investors in 1914 it is only because Argentine securities were so popular and well held on the Continent. British immigration into Argentina, although of a higher class and better supplied than most, was only a tiny fraction of the mass. Argentine loans, national, provincial and municipal, found eager buyers on the Continent. In 1907, Argentine Gold Bonds for £7 million were shared between London, Paris and Berlin; only 30 per cent of the £10 million Public Works Loan of 1909 was issued in London and the rest in Paris, Berlin and New York; the 70 million gold pesos (£14 million) Internal Gold Loan of 1911 was issued just in Paris and Antwerp.[86] Canadian loans, on the other hand, were floated in London alone, and Argentina's public debt was held more internationally. Argentine railways were particularly popular on the Continent. The French, said Yves Guyot, had invested several billion francs (at 25 francs to £1 sterling) in Argentina and Brazil.[87]

All the same, as much as 85 per cent of the £253 million invested in Argentine railways might have been British in 1913,[88] while the Argentine railway network was growing between 1907 and 1914 at an annual average of 1100 miles.[89] Argentine issues suffered like all others in the depression of 1913, although it is interesting that amidst general stagnation a small Argentine Government issue of £1 million (Port of Buenos Aires) went off quickly in London that April.[90] Another, brought out in August for the city of Buenos Aires, was not even underwritten; it was well received, largely oversubscribed, and subsequently reached a premium.[91] The abdication of the Chinese Emperor in 1912, the Balkan Wars of 1912–13, and the perpetual disasters of Mexico's Revolution, all helped to direct business the way of a politically stable, prosperous and progressing Argentina. In 1914, an Argentine Republic that could borrow freely abroad at 4½ per cent 'enjoyed a credit exceeded by none except the old creditor nations of Europe',[92] and in practice it took more new capital from London in 1914 than any other foreign country. Argentina was growing more rapidly between 1870 and 1914 than Australia. Nowadays we ask why Argentina lags behind Australia; in 1914, we would have asked the opposite;[93] much had happened since the sad autumn of 1890 when the *Economist* had warned that whatever good things were still to be had from Chile and Brazil, it would be better for British investors as a whole if they took their capital out of South America altogether.[94]

Canada, for the *British* investor, was better still. Here was the ideal destination for investment without significant competition from the Continent (although Canada was well within the range of US investment, usually industrial and direct). For the decade before the war Canada, a British Dominion that attracted British immigrants, offered special opportunities to British investors, and it is a tribute to the strength and attractions of Argentina that for a few years before the war Argentina was *more* popular with the mass of investors, British and foreign, than Canada, itself the most popular of the British Dominions.

The volume of portfolio investment that swept into Canada at the time was astonishing. Improvements in mining technology, in the techniques of wheat production, and in rail transport opened the Canadian West. Matthew Simon has calculated that during the half century before the war, British investors subscribed as much as £411 million in new Canadian issues, 'slightly more than ten per cent of the aggregate overseas securities of £4082 million they acquired'.[95] This is, of course, an aggregate – a 'flow' figure – and it omits both direct investment and the 'ebb' of ownership through the secondary market. Yet for these reasons it is more in line with Paish's estimates than mine.

However, these large sums for foreign investment in Canada were principally supplied in Britain, and they have been assumed to be wholly the case by Jacob Viner and his near contemporaries.[96] This was not quite true, although nearly so. An important exception was the Canadian Pacific Railways Co., the largest railway system in

Canada, which was a favourite with Canadians themselves and with every bourse in Europe; it was 'largely dealt in in New York' and 'very largely' in Berlin, so that one contemporary handbook classed Canadian Pacifics as belonging to the 'American Market' and as 'one of the most notable instances of an international stock'.[97]

Canada, Argentina and Australia were staple economies – wheat and forest products from Canada, grain and beef from Argentina, and wool, grain and non-ferrous metals from Australia. Canada was later to develop either than Australia or Argentina.[98] But both Canada and Argentina, unlike Australia, showed a thirst for imported capital. The savings of Canada (and of Argentina, too) were 'altogether inadequate' for the speed of development to which it aspired.[99] Canada borrowed too quickly and too much. Canadians themselves were reluctant holders of stocks and bonds before 1914.[100] The Dominion borrowed in London when, as the amazing mobilisation of Canadian resources during the war was to show, it could have raised its requirements at home at little or no extra cost. The price was saturation and distrust. Canada's borrowing fell off towards the end of 1911; only 10 per cent of a £7 million issue of Canadian Northern Guaranteed Stock was taken by the public.[101] Fifty per cent of a £5 million Canadian loan was left in the hands of the underwriters in February 1912.[102] No Canadian public institution could borrow at 4 per cent in 1913, and even Montreal, 'the first city of the Dominion', had to pay a full 4½ per cent.[103]

Canada came again into the market early in 1914, taking the 'lion's share of the total colonial applications'. New capital applications for Canada in London, in 1914, amounted to £45.4 millions; Australasian and Argentine applications were the closest at £19.4 million and £15 million respectively.[104] The figures showed where (in general) the market's tastes lay, but new Canadian issues were no longer fully subscribed. Seventy-eight per cent of a Canadian Government loan of £5 million (March 1914) was left with its underwriters.[105] When another government loan, also for £5 million, was issued in June 1914, the underwriters took back 88 per cent, which the *Economist* found unsurprising 'in view of the recent troubles affecting Canadian securities'.[106]

Neither the Paish/Stone figures for Argentina nor the Paish/Viner figures for Canada,[107] whatever their rights and wrongs as a measure of capital 'flows', can be said accurately to represent 'stock'. However, within the geographical distribution that I am now suggesting for Britain's stock of investment overseas in August 1914, the pace of change, the heavy rise in population in these regions of recent European settlement, and the great demand for imported capital, suggest that large numbers are more appropriate for Argentina and Canada than for many of those already appearing on the lists. Table 5.2 above indicates how for London issues of 1908–13, Canada outclassed all others. Argentina's 'new issues' on the London Stock Exchange lagged behind the United States, but they remained well ahead of the next borrower on the list, Brazil, even after the short-lived expansion of foreign lending to Brazil in 1911–12.

It is surely no surprise that the geographical spread of Britain's 'stock' of investment overseas in August 1914 was significantly different from the distribution to be expected from computed, aggregate 'flows' since the 1860s. Paish's own figures for 1908–13, and the matching numbers in the *Investor's Monthly Manual* (Table 5.2), have shown this to be the case. One can agree with Matthew Simon's aggregates over half a century; it is when he claims a 'remarkable stability', both in the type of investment and in its geographical distribution, that doubt stirs.[108]

## Notes

1. Paish (1911) pp. 176, 181.
2. Herbert Feis, *Europe, the World's Banker* (New York, 1930) p. 23.
3. A. K. Cairncross, *Home and Foreign Investment, 1870–1913* (Cambridge, 1953) p. 185.
4. J. H. Lenfant, 'British Capital Export, 1900–1913' (unpublished Ph.D. thesis, University of London, 1949) pp. 245–75.
5. A. R. Hall, *The London Capital Market and Australia, 1870–1914* (Canberra, 1963) p. 11.
6. M. Edelstein, 'The Determinants of UK Investment Abroad, 1870–1913: The US Case', *Journal of Economic History*, XXXIV, 4 (Dec. 1974) p. 982.
7. Karl Erich Born, *International Banking in the 19th and 20th Centuries* (Leamington Spa, trans. 1983) p. 118. This simple view cannot survive the work now being done by Lance Davis and Robert A. Huttenback, the first portion of which is published in the *Journal of Imperial and Commonwealth History*, XIII, 3 (May 1985) pp. 28–76.

8. Paish (1909), discussion p. 493.
9. 'London Stock Exchange Investments in Various Parts of the British Empire', *Economist*, 21 June 1911, p. 1344.
10. H. Feis, *Europe the World's Banker*, p. 25.
11. Philip S. Bagwell and G. E. Mingay, *Britain and America 1850–1939: A Study of Economic Change* (1970) p. 105–6.
12. A. J. H. Latham, *The Depression and the Developing World, 1914–1938* (1981) p. 67.
13. B. L. Anderson, 'Institutional Investment before the First World War: The Union Marine Insurance Company 1897–1915', in Sheila Marriner (ed.), *Business and Businessmen: Studies in Business, Economic and Accounting History* (Liverpool, 1978) pp. 57–8.
14. W. T. Jackson, *The Enterprising Scot: Investors in the American West after 1870* (Edinburgh, 1968) pp. 268–9, 276–7.
15. L. Davis, 'The Investment Market, 1870–1914: The Evolution of a National Market', *Journal of Economic History*, XXV, 3 (Sept. 1965) p. 392.
16. L. Davis, 'The Capital Markets and Industrial Concentration: The US and UK, a Comparative Study', *Economic History Review*, 2nd ser. XIX, 2 (1966) p. 271.
17. 'Foreign Municipal Issues', *Economist*, 25 Oct. 1913, p. 880.
18. Matthew Simon, 'The Pattern of New British Portfolio Investment 1865–1914', in J. H. Adler (ed.), *Capital Movements and Economic Development* (New York, 1967) pp. 43–4.
19. Robert Kindersley, 'British Overseas Investments in 1934 and 1935', *Economic Journal* (Dec. 1936) pp. 655–6.
20. J. M. Keynes underlines the point in his 'Foreign Investment and National Advantage', *Nation and the Athenaeum*, 2 August 1924.
21. *The Times*, 31 Dec. 1908, 12c.
22. Kindersley, 'British Overseas Investment in 1934 and 1935', p. 647.
23. George J. Holmes, *The Investors' Blue Book for 1914* (published by the *Investors' Chronicle*, 1914) p. 11.
24. *Investors' Monthly Manual* (June 1913) p. 286.
25. *Economist*, 3 Jan. 1914, p. 8.
26. 'The Stock Exchange Year', ibid., p. 5.
27. Percy F. Martin, 'Investments in Mexico – Are They Safe?', *Financial Review of Reviews* (March 1913) p. 21.
28. I. Stone, 'British Direct and Portfolio Investment in Latin America before 1914', *Journal of Economic History*, XXXVII, 3 (Sept. 1977) p. 695. Stone's short note on new UK issues for Argentina, 1865–1914, based on Matthew Simon's data, is rather more useful: 'British Investment in Argentina', *Journal of Economic History*, XXXII (June 1972) p. 546, although Simon's compilations differ rather alarmingly from the *Economist*'s 'new issues' for the same period.
29. Feis, *Europe the World's Banker*, p. 23 and fn. 21 (he must have meant portfolio, since this is the convention in his other figures).
30. Malcolm Falkus, 'Aspects of Foreign Investment in Tsarist Russia', *Journal of European Economic History*, 8, 1 (Spring 1979) p. 19.

31. 'The Collapse of Russian Securities', *Economist*, 25 July 1906, pp. 1247–8.
32. *Economist*, 9 Dec. 1907, p. 1970.
33. Ibid. 21 Oct. 1905, p. 1670.
34. Y. Guyot, 'The Amount, Direction and Nature of French Investments', in E. M. Patterson (ed.), *America's Changing Investment Market* (Philadelphia, 1916) p. 51.
35. H. Barkai, 'The Macro-Economics of Tsarist Russia in the Industrialization Era: Monetary Developments, the Balance of Payments and the Gold Standard', *Journal of Economic History*, XXXIII, 2 (June 1973) p. 363. It is not a view shared by William L. Blackwell who believes (perhaps wrongly) that foreign capital controlled as much as a third of Russian industry by 1900: Blackwell (ed.), *Russian Economic development from Peter the Great to Stalin* (New York, 1974) p. xxvii.
36. H. G. Moulton, *Japan: An Economic and Financial Appraisal* (1932) pp. 274, 495. Moulton was executive president of the Brookings Institution.
37. Royal Institute of International Affairs, *The Problem of International Investment* (1937) p. 122.
38. 'New Capital Issues and Prices', *Economist*, 4 July 1914, p. 6.
39. David Sheppard, *The Growth and Role of UK Financial Institutions, 1880–1962* (1971) p. 12.
40. Ian M. Drummond, *British Economic Policy and the Empire, 1919–1939* (1972) pp. 28–9.
41. Report of the Committee of Finance and Industry, June 1931: (British) *Parliamentary Papers*, 1930/31, XIII, para. 384, p. 389.
42. Robert Kindersley, 'British Overseas Investments in 1933 and 1934', *Economic Journal* (Sept. 1935) p. 445.
43. *Stock Exchange Official Intelligence* (1914), p. lxxxiv.
44. N. G. Butlin, 'Some Perspectives of Australian Economic Development, 1890–1965', in C. Forster (ed.), *Australian Economic Development in the Twentieth Century* (1970) p. 282.
45. Neville Cain, 'Trade and Economic Structure at the Periphery: The Australian Balance of Payments, 1890–1965', in ibid., p. 98.
46. Second Interim Report of the Dominions Royal Commission: *Parliamentary Papers*, 1914, XVIII, p. 186. The Minutes of Evidence are in *Parliamentary Papers*, 1914, XVII (QQ. 6485–6558 and p. 675).
47. 'The Finances of New South Wales', *Economist*, 21 Oct. 1893, p. 1259.
48. C. G. F. Simkin, *The Instability of a Dependent Economy: Economic Fluctuations in New Zealand, 1840–1914* (1951) pp. 198–9.
49. I. M. Drummond, 'Capital Markets in Australia and Canada, 1895–1914' (unpublished Ph.D. thesis, Yale University, 1959) p. 67.
50. Gordon Wood, *Borrowing and Business in Australia: A Study of the Correlation between Imports of Capital and Changes in National Prosperity* (1930) p. 153.
51. Vernon Lovell Phelps, *The International Economic Position of Argentina* (Philadelphia, 1938) pp. 118–19.
52. G. M. Meier, 'Economic Development and the Transfer Mechanism:

Canada, 1895–1913', *Canadian Journal of Economics and Political Science*, XIX, 1 (Feb. 1953) p. 3.

53. Drummond, 'Government Securities on Colonial New Issue Markets: Australia and Canada, 1895–1914', *Yale Economic Essays*, I, 1 (Spring 1961) p. 137.
54. *Economist*, 28 Oct. 1930, p. 700.
55. J. M. Keynes to the Editor, *Economist*, 27 Feb. 1909, p. 454.
56. 'Investments in India', ibid. 27 May 1911, p. 1124.
57. A. G. Chandavarkar, 'Money and Credit, 1858–1947', in Dharma Kumar (ed.) *The Cambridge Economic History of India* (Cambridge, 1983) p. 798.
58. R. O. Christensen, 'The State and Indian Railway Performance 1870–1920, Part II. The Government, Rating Policy and Capital Funding', *Journal of Transport History*, 3rd ser. 3, 1 (March 1982) p. 31.
59. *Economist*, 2 Aug. 1897, p. 1217.
60. G. F. Shirras, 'The Situation in India – a Rejoinder', *Economic Journal*, XLII (1932) pp. 572–3, in answer to Birla's article in ibid., pp. 485–9; Rao, 'The Indian Balance of Trade', ibid., XLIII (1933) pp. 169–71; exchanges in ibid. pp. 532–4. There is an intelligent discussion of the difficulties of estimating in 'British Capital Invested in India', *Statist*, 2 Sept. 1939, p. 282. A reputable, pre-war authority is Y. S. Pandit, *India's Balance of Indebtedness, 1898–1913* (London, 1937), although Pandit's preferred figure for British capital invested in India at the end of 1910–11 (59 100 *lakhs* of rupees), which was taken from H. F. Howard, is actually rather higher than Paish's estimate (54 780 *lakhs*) for both India and Ceylon combined (Pandit, pp. 1119–20).
61. A. J. H. Latham, *The International Economy and the Underdeveloped World, 1865–1914* (1978) p. 55.
62. Paish (1911), pp. 178–9.
63. S. Herbert Frankel, *Capital Investment in Africa: Its Cause and Effects* (1938) p. 204.
64. Ibid., pp. 149–50.
65. D. Hobart Houghton, 'Economic Development, 1865–1965', in Monica Wilson and Leonard Thompson (eds), *The Oxford History of South Africa*, II (1971) pp. 11, 18.
66. A. Emil Davies, *Investments Abroad* (Chicago, 1927) p. 10.
67. M. J. Bonn, 'The Nationalization of Capital', in Patterson, *America's Changing Investment Market*, p. 256.
68. R. Kubicek, 'Finance Capital and South African Goldmining, 1886–1914', *Journal of Imperial and Commonwealth History*, III, 3 (May 1975) p. 387.
69. *Economist*, 27 Jan. 1906, p. 123.
70. Kubicek, 'Finance Capital and South African Goldmining', p. 387.
71. Paish (1911) p. 178.
72. *Economist*, 21 June 1911, p. 1345.
73. *Stock Exchange Official Intelligence* (1914) p. lxxxiv.
74. R. Nurkse, 'International Investment Today in the Light of Nineteenth Century Experience', *Economic Journal* (Dec. 1954) pp. 748–50.

75. William P. Kennedy, 'Institutional Response to Economic Growth: Capital Markets in Britain to 1914', in Leslie Hannah (ed.), *Management Strategy and Business Development* (1976) p. 174.
76. Financial Times, *Investors' Guide for 1913* (1913), pp. 73–4.
77. S. J. Nicholas, 'British Multinational Investment before 1939', *Journal of European Economic History*, 11, 3 (Winter 1982) p. 626.
78. D. C. M. Platt, 'Canada and Argentina: The First Preference of the British Investor, 1904–1914', *Journal of Imperial and Commonwealth History*, XIII, 3 (May 1985) pp. 77–92.
79. H. Gordon Ross, 'A Local Appreciation of Argentina', *Financial Review of Reviews* (July 1913) p. 406.
80. Ernesto Tornquist & Co. Ltd, *The Economic Development of the Argentine Republic in the Last Fifty Years* (Buenos Aires, 1919) pp. 22–3.
81. Roberto Cortés Conde, 'Some Notes on the Industrial Development of Argentina and Canada in the 1930s', in D. C. M. Platt and Guido di Tella (eds), *Argentina, Australia and Canada: Studies in Comparative Development, 1870–1965* (1985) p. 151.
82. Carlos F. Díaz Alejandro, 'Argentina, Australia and Brazil before 1929', in ibid. pp. 98, 103.
83. Quoted in Carl Solberg, 'Land Tenure and Land Settlement: Policy and Patterns in the Canadian Prairies and the Argentine Pampa, 1880–1930', in ibid. p. 64.
84. David Rock, 'The Argentine Economy, 1890–1914: Some Salient Features', in Guido di Tella and D. C. M. Platt (eds), *The Political Economy of Argentina, 1880–1946* (1985) p. 69.
85. Solberg, 'Land Tenure and Land Settlement', p. 57, tables 3.2 and 3.3.
86. Harold E. Peters, *The Foreign Debt of the Argentine Republic* (Baltimore, 1934) p. 48.
87. Guyot, 'The Amount, Direction and Nature of French Investments', p. 52.
88. A. G. Ford, 'British Investment and Argentine Economic Development, 1880–1914', in David Rock (ed.), *Argentina in the Twentieth Century* (1975) p. 18, fn. 3.
89. Rock, 'Argentine Economy, 1890–1914', p. 66.
90. *Economist*, 19 Apr. 1913, p. 941.
91. Ibid., 23 Aug. 1913, pp. 385, 391; ibid. 30 Aug. 1913, p. 430; *Financial News*, 31 Dec. 1913, p. 6.
92. Peters, *Foreign Debt*, pp. 48–9.
93. Ezequiel Gallo, 'El Método Comparativo en Historia: Argentina y Australia (1850–1914)', in John Fogarty, Ezequiel Gallo and Héctor Dieguez, *Argentina y Australia* (Buenos Aires, 1979) pp. 7–9. The comparison is carried very much further in a recent book by Tim Duncan and John Fogarty, *Australia and Argentina on Parallel Paths* (Melbourne, 1984).
94. *Economist*, 6 Sept. 1890, p. 1137.
95. Simon, 'New British Investment in Canada, 1865–1914', *Canadian Journal of Economics*, III, 2 (May 1970) pp. 240, 248.

96. For example, Frank A. Knox, 'The Canadian Balance of Payments', in Herbert Marshall *et al.*, *Canadian–American Industry: A Study in International Investment* (New Haven, Conn., 1936) p. 304, fn. 12.
97. The General Securities Corporation, *The Investors' Handy Book of Active Stocks and Shares* (1913) p. xix.
98. The timing is explained very clearly in J. P. Fogarty's 'The Comparative Method in the Nineteenth Century Regions of Recent Settlement', *Historical Studies*, 19 (1981), passim.
99. Cairncross, *Home and Foreign Investment, 1870–1913*, p. 38.
100. Particularly informative in this context is Christopher Armstrong's 'Making a Market: Selling Securities in Atlantic Canada before World War I', *Canadian Journal of Economics*, XIII, 3 (Aug. 1980).
101. *Investors' Monthly Manual* (Dec. 1911) p. 696.
102. Ibid. (Feb. 1912) p. 63.
103. Ibid. (April 1913) p. 174.
104. *Economist*, 26 Dec. 1914, p. 1101.
105. Ibid. 7 March 1914, p. 617.
106. Ibid. 13 June 1914, p. 1467, and see also a leading article on 'Canadian Borrowing in London and the Credit of the Dominion', in the same issue, p. 1431.
107. Penelope Hartland, calculating on the basis of the balance of payments on current account for 1900–13, has reduced Viner's figures slightly in 'Canada's Balance of Payments since 1868', *Trends in the American Economy in the Nineteenth Century, Studies in Income and Wealth* (Princeton, N.J., 1960) p. 749. My point in drawing attention to this detail is simply to confirm that Viner and others have been compiling a figure for 'flows', not 'stock'. Jacob Viner's work on foreign investment in Canada is to be found in his influential *Canada's Balance of International Indebtedness, 1900–1913* (Cambridge, Mass., 1924); his total for British investment in Canada for 1900 to 1913 inclusive amounts to the equivalent of £350 million.
108. Simon, 'The Enterprise and Composition of New British Portfolio Foreign Investment, 1865–1914', *Journal of Development Studies*, 3, 3 (April 1967) pp. 280–92.

# 6 Second Thoughts on the Distribution by Function of British Investment

The distribution by function of British investment overseas on 31 December 1913, like its geographical distribution, is normally taken from Paish. The difficulties to be expected from the use of 'flow' figures as 'stock' for geographical distribution (the distribution of investment between nations) apply similarly to the distribution by function. Paish's figures have their imperfections, but if they are taken to mean what Paish originally intended, then the accumulated aggregates of annual investment in different occupational groups is a helpful guide to what happened to Britain's portfolio investment over the years. They are less useful in determining the distribution as it existed just before the First World War.

## PUBLISHED FIGURES AND THEIR PROBLEMS

Paish's estimates for distribution by function, December 1913, are shown in Table 6.1.

If this table, instead of representing aggregate investment under each heading over the years, were to be taken as 'stock' on 31 December 1913, the conclusions that might be drawn from it would be very different. Ragnar Nurkse understood the total in Feis (and hence in Paish) to represent capital 'outstanding', so that for him (and for many others) no less than 30 per cent of Britain's portfolio investment abroad in 1913 was in government stock and 40 per cent in railways.[1] The same partition of interests recurs, very generally, in the literature, and the notion that as much as 40 per cent was invested in railways is now well established.[2]

The percentage matters because it can lead to mysterious conclusions. Professor John Dunning, using the usual figures from Feis, found that in 1913 only 10 per cent of Britain's portfolio investment abroad took the form of minerals or raw material exploitation. This 10 per cent had 'the least beneficial effects on the development of the host countries apart from that of the export

*Table* 6.1 Paish's distribution of Britain's portfolio investment abroad, by function, 31 December 1913 (£ millions rounded to the nearest £100 000)

| | | | |
|---|---|---|---|
| *Goverments* | | | |
| National | | 675.5 | |
| Colonial | | 284.1 | |
| Municipal | | 147.5 | |
| | Total | | 1107.1 |
| *Railways* | | | |
| USA | | 616.6 | |
| Colonial | | 306.5 | |
| Indian | | 140.8 | |
| Other foreign | | 457.2 | |
| | Total | | 1521.1 |
| *Industry, Finance, Utilities etc.* | | | |
| Banks | | 72.9 | |
| Breweries | | 18.0 | |
| Commercial and industrial | | 145.3 | |
| Electric lighting and power | | 27.3 | |
| Financial, land and investment | | 244.2 | |
| Gas and water | | 29.2 | |
| Iron, coal and steel | | 30.5 | |
| Mines | | 272.8 | |
| Nitrate | | 11.6 | |
| Oil | | 40.6 | |
| Rubber | | 41.0 | |
| Tea and coffee | | 22.4 | |
| Telegraphs and telephones | | 43.7 | |
| Tramways | | 77.8 | |
| Others | | 9.2 | |
| | Total | | 1086.5 |
| | Grand Total | | 3714.7 |

*Source*: Paish (1914) p. vi.

enclaves which it creates'; the 40 per cent in railways, by contrast, was a contribution to 'one of the most powerful initiatives of growth' and most of the 30 per cent in government and municipal securities found its way into 'internal improvements and social overhead items'.[3]

The point is that whatever substance this kind of generalisation may have for the full period 1870 to 1914, the Paish/Feis figures are inadequate for the distribution by function of Britain's investment abroad as it stood in 1914. The difference is noticeable (see Table 6.2). Government securities, for the last years before the war, averaged 23 per cent, by contrast with the 26 per cent for which they were responsible over the last half century; railways averaged 35 per cent compared with 40.5 per cent; the proportion taken by 'Industry, Commerce, Finance and Utilities' had risen from 29.5 per cent to 34 per cent.

In the boom year 1910 the change in the public's attitude to the categories of foreign investment was at its most obvious (Table 6.2). 'Government', the share of which was in any case much swollen by *foreign* buying on the London market, accounted for only 19.5 per cent. 'Railways' took 32 per cent, a large part of which was again bought on foreign account. 'Industry, commerce, finance and utilities', to a much greater degree the sole property of *British* investors, took up no less than 43 per cent of London issues.

Admittedly, a single boom year on its own is not evidence enough. But whatever the year selected, it is only right to include Britain's 'direct' investment abroad in any realistic calculation of distribution by function. Precision is too much to expect, but if, for the sake of argument, I were to add £500 million of direct investment to Paish's £3.7 billion portfolio for 31 December 1913, the new distribution would show government loans at 23 per cent, municipal loans and utilities at 8 per cent, railways at 37 per cent, and commerce, finance, industry and others at 32 per cent.[4]

Table 6.2 below gives the figures, by function, for new issues from 1908 to 1913, and it indicates the pattern in capital applications on the London Stock Exchange for the last years before the war.

The figures are simply for portfolio investment. Sir Robert Kindersley, using Paish's distribution for 1907, showed that at the earlier period as much as three-quarters of British investment abroad took the form of government, municipal and railway securities. The proportion at just over 70 per cent in 1907 had fallen even by 1913, and by the late thirties the same group in Kindersley's new estimates

*Table* 6.2 Distribution by function of new issues in London, 1908–13 (major divisions, £ millions rounded to nearest £100 000)

| | *1908* | *1909* | *1910* | *1911* | *1912* | *1913* | *Total* |
|---|---|---|---|---|---|---|---|
| *Government and Railways* | | | | | | | |
| Government | 38.1 | 51.9 | 38.0 | 32.4 | 26.0 | 54.9 | 241.3 |
| Municipalities | 10.1 | 15.8 | 11.2 | 7.0 | 16.9 | 23.3 | 84.3 |
| Railways | 68.3 | 45.2 | 62.4 | 56.8 | 62.0 | 65.2 | 359.9 |
| Total | 116.5 | 112.9 | 111.6 | 96.2 | 104.9 | 143.4 | 685.5 |
| *Industry, Commerce, Finance and Utilities* | | | | | | | |
| Banks | 2.8 | 0.6 | 1.7 | 3.4 | 5.9 | 2.8 | 17.2 |
| Commercial, industrial etc. | 5.8 | 8.4 | 10.5 | 15.3 | 10.8 | 16.5 | 67.3 |
| Electric light and power | 1.2 | 2.4 | 3.1 | 4.8 | 5.4 | 3.0 | 19.9 |
| Financial, land, invested and trust | 8.9 | 4.9 | 13.5 | 11.2 | 11.1 | 5.3 | 54.9 |
| Iron, coal, steel and engineering | 1.0 | 2.4 | 4.4 | 1.4 | 6.5 | 2.5 | 18.2 |
| Mines | 5.1 | 8.3 | 10.8 | 8.9 | 5.7 | 3.8 | 42.6 |
| Oil | .8 | 2.4 | 10.5 | 3.8 | 6.4 | 5.7 | 29.6 |
| Rubber | .8 | 5.8 | 20.8 | 4.3 | 2.7 | 1.4 | 35.8 |
| Telephones and telegraph | 0.2 | 3.4 | 2.6 | 1.0 | 2.4 | 1.6 | 11.2 |
| Tramways | 3.9 | 10.7 | 4.3 | 5.6 | 12.1 | 4.5 | 41.1 |
| Others | 1.9 | 3.5 | 0.9 | 2.5 | 2.8 | 3.1 | 14.6 |
| Total | 32.4 | 52.8 | 83.1 | 62.2 | 71.8 | 50.2 | 352.4 |
| Grand Total | 148.9 | 165.7 | 194.7 | 158.4 | 176.7 | 193.6 | 1037.9 |

*Source*: Paish (1914) p. vi.

was down to a half. Kindersley's conclusion was that overseas investments since the war had changed their constitution and that they now included a large proportion of industrials.[5] The whole process was accelerated, no doubt, by the war, but it had begun well before.

Obviously, much of this difference is to be accounted for by the direct investment to which I have just referred. Paish's estimate for Britain's total investment abroad in finance and land, taken over half a century, was only £244 million, but then he was recording 'portfolio' investment when so much of this class of investment was in practice 'direct'.[6] Matthew Simon found from his annual estimates, wholly portfolio from London Stock Exchange issues, that only 4.8 per cent of new British investment abroad from 1906 to 1913 went into manufacturing,[7] yet industrial finance was almost always direct. Furthermore, if interpreted simply as portfolio, no account is taken of retained earnings nor of the interest that British individuals, financial institutions or commercial houses may have had in local manufacturing. Nor did it incorporate home-based manufacturing companies that built branch plants behind foreign tariff barriers. Direct investment that did not touch the stock exchange was a more powerful source of industrial finance than portfolio, at home certainly, but similarly abroad.

It is no more surprising that the pattern of investment by *function* should have shifted over the years than that it had by location. New forms of investment appeared on Paish's list that reflected gold mining in South Africa and Western Australia in the 1890s, the rubber boom in Brazil and the oil booms in Russia and Rumania, traction and power in Latin America, tea plantations in India and Ceylon, Malayan rubber plantations and Bolivian and Malayan tin. British investment in Malayan rubber reached a peak of £8.0 million authorised capital issues in 1910 – small beer, perhaps, but then plantation rubber had barely existed in 1908 and investment was down again to less than £1 million by 1913;[8] Paish calculated new issues in London in 1910 at £20.8 million. Admittedly, there is much to be said for Britton and Kennedy's opinion that 'British [investment] resources were mobilised to exploit and develop new technological possibilities inefficiently and in small quantities', for which blame is attached to the limitations imposed by a traditional and unique system of financial intermediation.[9] Yet it would be surprising if a market like London, so uniquely experienced, well equipped and fully informed, should have turned its back entirely on change.

Railways form the largest part in Paish's estimates – just over 40 per cent of Britain's portfolio investment overseas by the end of 1913. Earlier, Paish had explained that if allowance were made for the fact that so much railway finance was mobilised indirectly in the shape of government loans, the percentage of British foreign investment employed in the construction and operation of railways was over 60 per cent.[10]

Without doubt, railways were immensely important in Britain's overseas investment, and they remained so for decades. In spite of a turn in the tide against them, by the early 1930s they still accounted for nearly a quarter of Britain's investment worldwide – and that is before any allowance had been made for the proportion of government borrowing applied to the financing of railway construction.[11]

Yet railway securities were popular also with domestic investors and, like government stock, they returned home in large quantities. Railway companies were often overambitious, and many failed. Fraud and the 'watering' of capital were widely practised. Failed issues, like a large £10 million Canadian Pacific Railway Loan in 1914 (which alone made up more than half of the total for Colonial and Indian railways for the six months), were quoted for the whole amount in the *Economist*'s figures, although unsuccessful in London and in any case partly subscribed abroad. Huge figures for Britain's investment in railways (£1½ billion for 1913) must therefore be treated with caution.

## BRITISH INVESTORS AND THE STOCK OF US RAILWAY SECURITIES, AUGUST 1914

It would be unrealistic, within this one chapter, to attempt an analysis of the distribution of British investment for whatever purpose worldwide. But the story of what happened to US railway securities, the largest single category by far, illustrates the main points. US 'rails' have all the ingredients – enthusiastic exaggeration, fraud, speculation, boom, transnational marketing, advertisement and wartime propaganda. Such estimates as we have for British holdings of US rails have always been large, and in an unrefined form they do strange things to capital 'flows' and 'stock'. The nominal value of US railway securities quoted in London at the end of 1913 was over £1.7 billion, of which £800 million was in stocks and shares and £900 million in bonds.[12] The total capital outstanding in US rails at home and abroad, in June 1914, was over £4 billion ($20.2 billion).[13]

It is anyone's guess what these gigantic figures actually mean. During the most active stage of railway expansion – the early 1870s and then again during the early 1880s – stock 'watering' was endemic and 'scrip dividends' of up to 100 per cent were paid out to shareholders on some of the larger lines. Henry Villard, George Pullman, Collis Huntington, Jay Gould and Samuel Sloan were names only too familiar to an unfortunate generation of European investors, as they were to the citizens of the United States; Huntington's great projects succeeded with the aid of the earning power of the Central Pacific and its ability to raise millions of dollars in stocks and bonds. These were heady amounts, but in Paish we are faced with a figure of £616.6 million for Britain's portfolio investment in US railways in December 1913, and the estimate has come to be accepted as 'stock' by such authorities is Leland Jenks[14] and Cleona Lewis.[15] It can be imagined what such a sum has done to Paish's distributions. Within his geographical distribution, Paish's figure for railways contributed very nearly 82 per cent of his total for British investment in the United States, and left the United States in December 1913 nearly £240 million ahead of Canada, its nearest competitor. Yet the Kindersley estimate for Britain's holding of every variety of quoted US securities in London by the end of 1936 was only £81 million.[16] British investment in the United States had declined, but could the difference have been so great?

The truth is that whatever the real enthusiasm for US 'rails' that most certainly existed with British investors in the 1870s and 1880s, the panic in New York of 1893, and the wreck of US railway finances, brought both heavy sales and the end of further buying on the London market. Even before, during the Baring crisis of 1890–1 (a London affair), huge quantities of US railway stocks and bonds were either dumped in New York or sold by Britons to Frenchmen at discounts of 7 to 9 per cent on boom prices.[17]

The return of US securities to the home country in the 1890s and early 1900s was widely discussed. Alexander Noyes described Europe as 'practically drained of American stocks and bonds' by 1900.[18] The 'glory had departed' from the Yankee Market on the London Stock Exchange,[19] and it showed little sign of real recovery until the mid-1900s. Sir Robert Giffen recognised (in 1901) that Britain had lately been parting with certain kinds of international securities 'especially American',[20] and a sympathiser in the *Contemporary Review* explained that Britain by now had sold nearly the whole amount of its 'immense holdings' of American rails.[21]

Both Giffen and the *Contemporary Review* were promoting a political cause, but Edgar Crammond may have been more nearly right when he discovered that of the £1.3 billion American railroad shares and bonds quoted in the London list for 1907, those held in

Britain could 'barely exceed one fourth', put more precisely at £330 million.[22] Lenfant later explained that the weight of evidence pointed to conventional overstatement of foreign investment outstanding in the United States in 1908,[23] by which time New York itself was showing signs of re-emergence from the banking crisis of 1907.

Nobody could have been surprised. Before the 'panic', respectable financial journals like the *Statist* and the *Economist* had been enthusiastic promoters of investment in 'well-secured', underpriced US railway bonds; they became firm and implacable critics thereafter. But US rails had been underpriced for good reason. 'Officials in the United States,' said the *Economist* in November 1893, 'have deliberately gone out of their way to destroy the small remains of confidence that European investors still have in Yankee rails'; there was a conspiracy of silence in big concerns like the Erie Company, owned mainly in Britain, in dispute with other British-owned companies such as the New York, Pennsylvania and Ohio: in too many cases US railway shares were mere gambling counters, 'or rather perhaps, loaded dice'.[24] It was little better a quarter of a century later when Hartley Withers, by now himself editor of the *Economist*, commented on the 'glorious game of make-believe' in railway accounts home and foreign, the 'tricks of legerdemain', the complete uncertainty that confronted all enquirers when they tried to get at the facts behind the figures.[25]

The sale of US railway securities in London experienced short revivals in 1897 and in the last months of 1906 (when the amount sold in London was said to have exceeded £10 million); there is reason to believe, however, that the 1906 sales were merely temporary, and that the shares found their way back to New York.[26] This was a pessimistic opinion from Edgar Crammond, but the *Economist* had found the same. Its estimate for the balance of British purchases of American railway and industrial shares in 1906 was £8 million; like Crammond, it explained that a large proportion of the purchases for the latter part of the year had recently found their way back to the United States.[27] Massive buying genuinely took place in 1910, when about £40 million was issued in European markets.[28] But sales were right down again in 1911 so that by the third quarter they were smaller for all London issues together than they had been since the same period in 1906; British investors were turning more towards the lower-yielding securities of the United Kingdom.[29]

Throughout the entire period since 1893, US rails were always in some demand on 'the Street', although not in the London Exchange itself; it was sometimes little more than a matter of timing, since the main market, New York, had been at work for less than an hour when London's 'official' Exchange closed. But distrust was lasting. Midway through 1908, American securities were described as completely neglected in London.[30] In 1909, *The Times* explained that dealings were confined almost entirely to 'a small circle of bold professionals', big operators of whom the public knew nothing.[31] There was great activity, but much of it even in the boom year of 1910 was merely arbitrage on US railroad shares and bonds, and speculation by brokers on the New York Exchange.[32] Conservative opinion was still 'on the whole suspicious' of US rails.[33] In spite of an improvement later that year (1910), a leader writer in the *Economist*, during the summer of 1911, described US railway shares as 'only a danger signal to the British investor' whose attention continued to be restricted to a few old favourites like the Illinois, Pennsylvania and New York Central.[34] The Pennsylvania Railway had been described by *The Times* in 1908 as recognised for many years as the standard for sound investment in Britain.[35] Yet in 1914, after all the excitement of the intervening years, the *Financial Review of Reviews* was still trying to persuade reluctant British investors to be less suspicious of US railways.[36] The period for the repurchase of US rails was in fact quite short. The *Financial News* discussed a number of reasons why, in 1913, they finished up nearer the bottom as a rule than the top, and invariably below the level obtaining twelve months before.[37] B. M. Anderson, writing in 1919, could find no evidence of a real boom at all in US rails in Europe since the financial panic of 1907,[38] and in the first four months of 1914 US issues of all kinds in London were down to less than half of the level for the first four months of 1912.[39]

It was not, then, an occasion on which Britons might have been expected fully to re-establish themselves as holders of US rails to the extent that whatever had been lost in the 1890s and early 1900s was restored by 1914. For US railways in particular there are immense problems even in identifying the nationality of investors. From the time that European investment picked up again in 1904, a very large part of the stocks of American railroads were issued in the form of 'bearer' bonds (bonds made out simply to bearer, without further identification). Bearer bonds, as it happened, were particularly favoured by Continental investors; they were easily negotiable, and they were marketable not only in London but in Paris, Berlin,

Amsterdam and other Continental Exchanges; they were described as passing from hand to hand, in and out of bankers' tin boxes – 'nowhere recorded in a manner which is accessible to the curious'.[40]

It is true that strong markets had existed for US rails on the Continent itself without reference to London – in Berlin, Frankfurt and Paris; they had done so since well back into the exciting years of the 1870s and 1880s. But London, even occasionally for America's domestic investors, was the most convenient of all. When the *Economist* reported the allotment of a large portion of Great Northern Railroad securities to London in 1905, it added that the issue would 'probably not draw very largely on *British* capital resources'.[41] This was quite evidently the case. Paish thought that beyond those large amounts of American securities sold direct, about a third of the new issues placed in London during the first half of 1906 was subscribed by the Continent.[42]

New York's banking crisis of 1907 reinforced the international role of the London market. It showed that French investors had already taken part in the market for all kinds of American securities on a scale unknown in the past, and they were reported even then (December 1907) as 'eager buyers of good US railway bonds through London'.[43] The *Statist*'s explanation was that France had never been as intimately connected with the United States as Britain, so that its investors looked to London for information and advice; besides, 'France [had] an immense accumulation of unemployed money'.[44]

This can only throw doubt on the estimates for 'British' holdings of US 'rails', derived as they are almost entirely from the record of purchases and sales on London's international market. Quite apart from the marked reluctance shown by Britons to repurchase US railway securities until as late as 1910, and even then only for one short, sharp burst, the identification of London issues with 'British' subscriptions is even less reliable for the bonds of US railways than it is for the mass of other international securities issued in London.

Fortunately, the existence of a British Government agency during the war charged with the mobilisation of British holdings of dollar securities gives us at least a clue to the kind of commitment of British investors to US rails in August 1914. Much legend and confusion have surrounded the operation of the Dollar Securities Committee, some of which was deliberate. The British Treasury has always been obsessively secretive. Everybody knew that dollar securities were crossing the Atlantic during the war, but nobody was allowed to know how much. W. R. Lawson, the author of a useful book on the management of Britain's war finances, told an American audience in 1916 that the British Treasury let it be known how agreeably surprised it was by the great volume of dollar bonds and securities sent in for sale on behalf of the war effort, but never gave the slightest hint of the actual amount. Only the vaguest clues were ever forthcoming, and they came from the New York press – the report of the arrival of an Atlantic liner with $25 million of securities aboard, or the reputed weakness in Wall Street sales on apprehension of selling on behalf of the British Treasury. About movements as a whole, Lawson complained, we were allowed to know as little as we were about those fabulous munitions contracts for which the dollar securities were supposedly intended to pay.[45]

There was every reason, quite apart from war policy and propaganda, to keep quiet on sales. Sales of securities to build up banking credits had to be made as unobtrusively as possible if prices were to be maintained.[46] C. K. Hobson, in an article published in Philadelphia in 1916, talked of 'a vast pouring back into the United States of American securities slowly accumulated during the past century', running into 'some hundreds of millions'.[47]

The temptation has been to conclude that the gap between Paish's huge figure of £617 million for British ownership of US railway securities, and the £28 million estimated as still held in Britain in 1930, was to be accounted for by the fact that railway securities were the principal element in the organised liquidation of dollar holdings during the war. This, in fact, is what is normally thought to have been the case. Conventionally, £1 billion of Britain's foreign securities were disposed of during the war, as explained both by J. M. Keynes and Sir Josiah Stamp.[48] The Chancellor of the Exchequer in his post-war Budget speech (1919) quoted a figure of about £1 billion for the sale of foreign securities, and it was this that was repeated subsequently by an 'official' source, the *Board of Trade Journal* of 15 January 1920.[49] Three years later, the *Board of Trade Journal* reported the more sophisticated total of £623 million of first-class securities requisitioned and *sold* by the Treasury, after which an additional £150 million needed to be written off as lost investment with belligerents.[50] Sir Robert Kindersley adopted the £623 million of this second account and compared it to the £600 million in Paish's 1907 estimate, from which he confirmed the liquidation of British interest in US rails during the war.[51] With such impressive authority, the figures have naturally found their way into the textbooks.

It is worth taking a closer look at the evidence. The British

Treasury brought organised pressure to bear on British holders of dollar securities to persuade them to sell their securities to the government or to deposit them on loan. The idea was first to provide dollars for use in war purchases, but it later became a sustained effort to support the pound/dollar exchange.

In July 1915, the Bank of England was instructed to buy US dollar securities in London, and to send them to New York. On 15 December, insurance and trust companies were requested to sell or to lend US securities to the Treasury, and on 31 December the general public was asked to do the same. An 'American Dollar Securities Committee' began work in January 1916 charged with the control of the operations begun by the Treasury. By now these were intended entirely to improve and maintain the rate of exchange – in which they were largely successful, since the rate of \$4.75 to £1 sterling was maintained up to the time that control was lifted (21 March 1919). Because of the disappointing results obtained simply by patriotic admonitions, the Chancellor of the Exchequer obtained authority from the House of Commons, on 29 May 1916, to impose an additional tax of two shillings in the £1 on the dividend to be received from such securities as the Treasury, by circulation of special lists, declared its willingness to buy, heavily increasing sales and deposits. On 16 June 1916, the deposit scheme was extended to holdings of less than \$5000, and on 12 August certain securities were included, other than US dollar securities, that had a ready market; registered Canadian and South American railway stocks were offered in quantity, amounting to about £170 million.

Nor was this the end of it. Pressure to submit was increased in September 1916, when the US Government imposed a tax of 1 per cent on US securities held by non-resident aliens, to be increased to 2 per cent from 1 January 1917. On 17 February 1917, the British Treasury decreed that owners or custodians of certain specified securities (dollars and others) should take steps effectively to deliver them to the Dollar Securities Committee on or before 17 March at prices specified against the securities.[52] Other measures were taken to tighten the vice over the next couple of years, although the entry of the United States into the war on 6 April 1917 reduced the immediate pressure, since the Allies were no longer under an obligation to deposit securities as collateral to loans and were asked only to deposit their own government bonds with the US Treasury. In practice, however, collateral schemes of one kind or another continued until after the war.[53]

The Dollar Securities Committee published its final report in 1919.[54] It listed all securities that had passed through its hands, and included the Treasury operations that had taken place before the Committee took responsibility on 1 January 1916. A total of £284.6 million in dollar securities was obtained, of which £184.5 million was purchased and £100.1 million received on loan. If non-railway securities are deducted, together with those dollar securities actually registered under Canada, Cuba etc., about £86 million must be removed from the combined total of sales and loans, so that the quantity held in US rails is reduced to £198.6 million. It is difficult to be precise – the transactions were large and the nature of the listed securities is not always entirely clear; an addition of £20.6 million must be made for sterling bonds acquired by the Committee in US rails. Nevertheless, the final total of US railway securities bought and loaned through the British Treasury during the war is unlikely to have risen much above £225 million.

This is far below Paish's £616 million. It includes a large portion of securities which, although held in London, were in reality the property of foreigners, and these, held particularly by Americans, must generally have returned to the United States under the Treasury's incentives and marketing arrangements. Furthermore, Paish's figures were taken from the reports of public companies listed on the London Stock Exchange, whereas Cleona Lewis has calculated that about 18 per cent of the dollar securities after 1896 listed in the Report of the Dollar Securities Committee were issued and quoted only in New York.[55] This could only mean that the very much smaller total revealed by the Committee's report actually included a sizeable portion that was not even registered in Paish. A conclusion might be that on the most generous interpretation of securities that missed the net, actual British holdings of US railway securities were unlikely to have been much more than a half of the amount calculated by Paish for the end of 1913.

Three points, however, need to be established. First, how effective was the Treasury in mobilising British holdings, either on its own or through the medium of the Dollar Securities Committee? Then, how many of Britain's dollar securities had crossed the Atlantic before the middle of 1915, when the Treasury began formally to act? Finally, did the prices of US rails in New York depreciate during the war, or did they maintain their value so that the amounts realised in sales could be said to represent at least some equivalent to the market value of those securities in August 1914?

1. Opinions on the effectiveness of Treasury action differ. In its early stages, for the first half of 1916, much opposition was expressed to this new manifestation of State control, focused most particularly on the Chancellor's imposition of an extra 10 per cent on income tax from 29 May. The subject was debated at length in the House of Commons on 27 June. But once the principle was accepted, and pressure had increased, receipts were considerable – patriotism, tax measures both in Britain and the United States, the sanction of the law, the attractive terms offered, all combined to make it unlikely that investors would hold back. In any case, much of Britain's stock of US rails was by now in the possession of financial institutions, and both insurance and trust companies had been asked to sell or lend their dollar securities to the Treasury from as early as December 1915; British joint stock banks are known to have disposed of the major part of what they had under the government scheme.[56] Altogether, it is likely that the greater part of US dollar securities held by Britons in August 1914 were sold or lent to the Treasury in the course of the war.

It may be that the interest of Cleona Lewis in establishing a large figure for British holdings in US rails has helped to persuade her that pressure on British investors was lifted in April 1917 (when the United States entered the war), only a month after penalties were imposed that might have mobilised the securities; her conclusion was that a considerable amount was therefore never registered with the Committee.[57] The evidence, such as it is, suggests the opposite.

2. No figure can be attached to those dollar securities that returned to the United States from Europe in the interval before registration began with the British Treasury in the summer of 1915. No doubt large quantities of dollar securities were resold to the United States right at the start of the war, but the likelihood is that the great majority during these first months came from the Continent. Panic sales in 1912, when Continentals unloaded their most realisable securities in London at the outbreak of war in the Balkans, had already shown what was likely to happen in a crisis. Continental investors sold up again in 1914, but this time in New York. The low prices to which US rails fell before Wall Street stopped trading were due, said the *Economist*, to 'great pressure to sell on the part of European (Continental) holders'.[58] Germans were deeply committed in US rails, as were many others on the Continent.

The reaction among *British* investors was far less immediate. The closure of the London Stock Exchange from 29 July to January 1915, war euphoria and the belief in 'peace by Christmas', the inexplicable (and temporary) fall in the US dollar in relation to sterling, meant that by the time sales were again to be contemplated, prospective sellers found themselves hedged around by a host of Treasury restrictions. The first major shipment of repatriated securities did not take place until August 1915, as a preliminary to the Anglo-French loan of October, and it was then that a partner in Morgans (who were handling the loan on behalf of the Allies) is reported to have found securities arriving in New York 'by the bale' to be snapped up by thrifty American investors.[59] But the Treasury was now on the watch and the transactions have been recorded.

In December 1915, when Professor Foxwell arrived independently at the idea of something like the Dollar Securities Committee, he explained that such an organisation was necessary because the movement of US securities back to the United States had been *impeded* so far, and sales greatly *obstructed* by the enforcement of Leeman's Act and the obstacles to arbitrage.[60] Hartley Withers, in a propaganda book on the virtues of international finance, implied that Britain's capital was little depleted by New Year's Eve, 1915 (just before the Dollar Securities Committee came into action), after which Britons sold Pennsylvania Railroad bonds to turn them into shells.[61] Ernest Ludlow Bogart, an American, could produce little evidence of any extensive return to US railway securities until the first half of 1916.[62] The Dollar Securities Committee, which recorded Treasury transactions from the middle of 1915, must therefore have taken account of the greater part.

3. It is obvious that if the prices of US rails on New York markets fell substantially during the First World War, the amounts realised by Treasury sales would not represent the true value of British investment in August 1914. Could it be that the difference between Paish's high figure and the much lower amount reported by the Dollar Securities Committee is explicable by a sharp fall in the market price?

Most US railways, even the best, had experienced a heavy decline in the price of their securities ever since the high point reached in 1906. The \$100 shares of Illinois Central fell from $188\frac{5}{8}$ (highest) in 1906 to $131\frac{3}{4}$ (highest) in 1913; Pennyslvania Railroad \$50 shares were $75\frac{3}{4}$ (highest) in 1906, and they were down to $63\frac{1}{2}$ (highest) in 1913.[63] The reopening of the New York Stock Exchange in December

1914 reversed the downward trend, and by the time of the 'munitions boom', in London, of the summer of 1915 they were healthy again.[64] It was at this point that the British Treasury came into the market.

US rails never shared in the enormous rise in US industrial stocks or in the 'fabulous war profits' of manufacturing industry. But railway securities appreciated modestly, 'the more noteworthy in view of the fact that it has occurred in the face of the heaviest foreign liquidation to which the American market has ever been subjected'.[65] Increased traffic created by the war was bound to affect the prices even if it did not in fact pick up until the early summer of 1915.[66] Continued realisation of European holdings, Continental and British, kept 'rails' from following 'industrials'. Corporate AAA bond prices (mainly railways) were slightly higher in 1916 than they were in 1914, but rather lower again in 1917 and lower still in 1918.[67] But the difference was not devastating, and by now the major liquidations through the British Treasury were already effected – in the second half of 1915, the whole of 1916 and the first quarter of 1917.

The inference must be that Britain's stock of US rails was not disposed of at panic prices, or even at more than moderate reductions, if at all, on the market value at which they stood in July 1914. The amount of US railway securities reported by the Dollar Securities Committee in 1919 is a reliable indication of value for at least the major part of British holdings before the war. Britons could not possibly have held £617 million in US railway securities just before the war, nor in consequence could railways have taken over 40 per cent of Britain's total portfolio overseas.

## CONCLUSIONS

It is more than unlikely that accurate numbers can ever be attached to the preferences of British investors as far back as August 1914. All the same, attitudes were unquestionably changing; they had been changing for a whole generation. The trend is visible even in standard, portfolio investment; it becomes much more evidently the case if account is taken of the 'direct' route preferred for so many of the newer classes of investment.

Averages on the aggregate of half a century's investment, the 'Paish method', disguise change, and British investors emerge as conservatives in pursuit of 'safe' returns in government stock and foreign railways. No doubt this was true of many. But the same is improbable as a general rule for what still remained the world's leading market for international securities, served by the best informed and most experienced of international Exchanges.[68]

**Notes**

1. R. Nurkse, 'International Investment Today in the Light of Nineteenth Experience', *Economic Journal* (Dec. 1954) p. 747.
2. Recently in the textbooks, but F. Lavington had accepted Paish's distribution by occupation back in the 1920s in *The English Capital Market* (1921) p. 186, as did J. H. Lenfant in 'British Capital Exports, 1900–1913' (unpublished Ph.D., University of London, 1949) pp. 245–75.
3. John H. Dunning, *Studies in International Investment* (1970) p. 18.
4. The £500 million for 'direct' investment is the figure suggested in my revision of Paish, chapter 1 of part II. I am assuming that 90 per cent (£450 million) can fairly be allocated to the categories 'commerce, finance, industry and others (including land)', and that the remaining 10 per cent (£50 million) was shared equally between railway securities bought outside the Stock Exchange and direct investment in public utilities, etc.
5. Sir Robert Kindersley, 'A New Study of British Foreign Investments', *Economic Journal*, XXXIX (March 1929) p. 21.
6. Paish (1914) p. vi.
7. M. Simon, 'The Enterprise and Industrial Composition of New British Portfolio Foreign Investment, 1855–1914', *Journal of Development Studies*, 3 (1966–7) pp. 288–9.
8. Richard T. Stillson, 'The Financing of Malayan Rubber, 1905–1923', *Economic History Review*, 2s. XXIV, 4 (1971) p. 594.
9. Rachel E. Britton and William P. Kennedy, 'The Industrial Mobilization of Great Fortunes in Victorian Britain: The Evidence from Scottish Probate Inventories, 1876–1913', unpublished paper, 10 March 1983, p. 31.
10. Paish (1911) p. 185.
11. Sir Robert Kindersley, 'British Overseas Investments in 1931', *Economic Journal* (June 1933) p. 202, also his article for overseas investments in 1934 and 1935 in ibid (Dec. 1936) pp. 658–9. The governments of Japan and China took particular responsibility in this respect.
12. *Stock Exchange Official Intelligence for 1914* (1914) p. 1707.
13. *Historical Statistics of the US: Colonial Times to 1970*, vol. II (Washington, 1975) p. 735.
14. L. H. Jenks, 'British and American Railway Development', *Journal of*

*Economic History,* XI, 4 (Fall, 1951) p. 375; also his 'Railroads as an Economic Force in American Development', ibid. IV, 1 (May, 1944) p. 9, where Jenks remarked that foreign ownership of US railroad securities might have reached as much as one-third of the total in 1890 and nearly as much just before 1914.

15. C. Lewis, *America's Stake in International Investments* (Washington, 1938) p. 119. Professor Lewis does not give her source, but the figure of $3.7 billion (£740 million) comes almost unaltered from Paish.
16. Sir Robert Kindersley, 'British Overseas Investments in 1935 and 1936', *Economic Journal* (Dec. 1937) pp. 655, 657.
17. C. P. Kindleberger, 'International Propagation of Financial Crises: The Experience of 1888–93', in Wolfram Engels *et al.* (eds), *International Capital Movements, Debt and Monetary System* (Mainz, n.d.) p. 229. Oscar Morgenstern cites M. Patron (1910) to the same effect, *International Financial Transactions and Business Cycles* (Princeton, 1959) p. 526.
18. A. Dana Noyes, *Forty Years of American Finance* (New York, 1909) p. 280.
19. Charles Duguid, *The Story of the Stock Exchange* (1901) pp. 250–1.
20. Sir Robert Giffen, 'The Expenditure of National Capital', *Journal of the Institute of Bankers*, XXII (June 1901) p. 255.
21. *Contemporary Review* (July 1901) p. 28.
22. E. Crammond, 'British Investments Abroad', *Quarterly Review* (July 1907) pp. 247–8.
23. Lenfant, 'British Capital Export', pp. 286, 288.
24. 'American Railways – Information Wanted', *Economist*, 11 Nov. 1893, pp. 1341–2.
25. H. Withers, *Stocks and Shares* (1917 edn) pp. 163–4
26. Crammond, 'British Investments Abroad', p. 269.
27. 'Anglo American Trade and Finance', *Economist*, 18 May 1907, p. 857.
28. *Statist*, 3 Dec. 1910, p. 1318.
29. *Economist*, 7 Oct. 1911, pp. 700–2.
30. *The Times*, 3 July 1908, p. 11f.
31. Ibid., 18 Aug. 1909, p. 13a; ibid. 24 Sept. 1909, p. 13f.
32. O. Morgenstern, *International Financial Transactions*, pp. 526–7.
33. *The Times*, Financial and Commercial Supplement, 14 Jan. 1910, p. 14e.
34. 'The Investment Markets', *Economist*, 26 Aug. 1911, p. 431. The substantial holdings, as revealed later in the Report of the Dollar Securities Committee, were in the Erie Railroad, the Atchinson Topeka and Sante Fe Railway, Baltimore & Ohio, Chesapeake & Ohio, Illinois Central, Kansas City Terminal Rly, Minneapolis St Paul and S.S. Marie Rly, New York Central and Hudson River R.R., Northern Pacific, Southern Pacific, Great Northern Rly Co., Pennsylvania R.R., and the Union Pacific. The list seems long until one realises that there were 194 US railway companies of more than 100 miles each in length in operation in 1914.
35. *The Times*, Financial and Commercial Supplement, 12 June 1908, p. 4a.

36. James Davenport Whelpley, 'American Investments', *Financial Review of Reviews* (Sept. 1914) p. 1051.
37. *Financial News*, 31 Dec. 1913, p. 6.
38. B. M. Anderson, *Effects of the War on Money, Credits and Banking in France and the United States* (New York, 1919) p. 143.
39. *Statist*, 2 May 1914, p. 241.
40. Withers, *Stocks and Shares*, pp. 45–6. The first edition of this book was published in 1910.
41. *Economist*, 30 Dec. 1905, p. 2110 (my italics).
42. 'Our Investments of New Capital', *Statist*, 9 July 1910, p. 68.
43. *Statist*, 21 Dec. 1907, p. 1170.
44. Ibid., 28 Dec. 1907, p. 1212.
45. W. R. Lawson, 'The British Treasury and the London Stock Exchange', in E. M. Patterson (ed.), *America's Changing Investment Market* (Philadelphia, 1916) p. 75.
46. Thomas Conway, 'Financing American War Orders', in ibid. p. 147.
47. C. K. Hobson, 'British Overseas Investments, Their Growth and Importance', *Annals of the American Academy of Political and Social Science* (1916) p. 34.
48. J. M. Keynes, *The Economic Consequences of the Peace* (1920) p. 258; J. Stamp, 'An Estimate of the Capital Wealth of the United Kingdom in Private Hands', *Economic Journal*, XXVIII, III (Sept. 1918) p. 286.
49. E. Victor Morgan, *Studies in British Financial Policy, 1914–25* (1952) p. 331.
50. *Board of Trade Journal*, CX, 29 March 1923, p. 385 (my italics).
51. Kindersley, 'A New Study of British Foreign Investments', *Economic Journal*, XXXIX (March 1929) pp. 9–10.
52. The history of the Treasury intervention is spelt out in the *Report of the American Dollar Securities Committee*: British Parliamentary Papers, 1919, XIII, pp. 524–5, 532.
53. These are explained by A. W. Kirkaldy in his contribution to the volume he edited: *British Finance During and After the War 1914–1921* (1921) pp. 177–88, 196.
54. *Parliamentary Papers*, 1919, XIII.
55. Lewis, *America's Stock in Industrial Investments* (Washington D.C., 1938) p. 40.
56. A. H. Gibson, 'Banking, Currency, War Finance, etc.', in A. W. Kirkaldy (ed.), *Industry and Finance* (1920) p. 117. Gibson was himself the brain behind the whole scheme for mobilising foreign securities, and had advocated it since July 1915.
57. Lewis, *America's Stock*, p. 543. She discusses British holdings of US rails in useful detail, pp. 529–57, although she seems to share the belief that Paish's accumulated figure was in fact a stock figure for the end of 1913 (ibid. pp. 531, 546). She also attaches rather more importance to Lorée's estimates than I would myself. L. F. Lorée was president of the Delaware & Hudson (Rly) Company. He made four enquiries altogether in 1915–17 in which he requested the president of each line of over 100 miles in length to return to him the amount of their securities standing

in the names of foreign owners. For 31 January 1915 he arrived at a par value of US securities held abroad of $2.7 billion (£540 million). The figures for all four of his enquiries are reproduced in Ernest Ludlow Bogart, *War Costs and Their Financing* (New York, 1921) p. 73. The prevalence of 'bearer' securities in US rails (by which actual identities were concealed), and the absence of distinction between the nationality of 'foreigners', make Lorée's returns unhelpful in the present context.

58. *Economist*, 28 Nov. 1914, p. 947.
59. Vincent P. Carosso, *Investment Banking in America: A History* (Cambridge, Mass., 1970) pp. 212–13.
60. H. S. Foxwell, 'British War Finance', *Economic Journal* (Dec. 1915), as reprinted in his *Papers on Current Finance* (1919) pp. 17, 30 and fn. 1 (my italics).
61. Withers, *International Finance* (1916) p. 279.
62. Bogart, *War Costs*, pp. 72–4.
63. *Stock Exchange Official Intelligence* (1914) p. 1710.
64. Lawson, 'The British Treasury', p. 86.
65. S. S. Huebner (Professor of Insurance and Commerce at the University of Pennsylvania), 'The American Security Market During the War', in Paterson, *America's Changing Investment Market*, pp. 89–102. This was a careful investigation, based on *Babson's*.
66. G. B. Anderson, 'The Effects of the War on New Security Issues in the United States', in ibid. pp. 127, 129.
67. Standard and Poor's prices and index as reprinted in the *Historical Statistics of the United States*, for which I am indebted to Dr Michie of the University of Durham.
68. It is in this respect that Ranald Michie's work, already published or now with the publisher, is proving so interesting.

# 7 Further Implications and Conclusions

Any reduction in British figures must entail at least some rethinking of the estimates for other capital exporters before the First World War. Contemporary France is generally acknowledged to have come closest to Britain as an investor abroad, with Germany not far behind. New York, for a few months in 1901, seemed to have captured the central position in international finance, and Wall Street was predicting that it was about to challenge London's supremacy; but long before the financial crisis of 1907 the United States was back to open borrowing on a very large scale, and New York's financial community was 'stretched flat on its back' in the panic of that year.[1]

## FRANCE AS AN INVESTOR ABROAD IN AUGUST 1914

The position of France (and of Paris in particular) is unclear; there are, indeed, 'très réelles incertitudes' about any global figure.[2] A range of estimates is quoted in Table 7.1 below, but it must be said that even if not specified as such, most of the estimates are quite clearly intended to show the aggregation of French investment abroad over the decades rather than the stock as held in August 1914. Even when a stock figure is actually indicated, as it is by Maurice Lévy-Leboyer, a comparison is then made between an amalgam of accumulated British 'flows' (from Paish, Feis and Imlah) and what is clearly intended to be stock for 1913.[3] The 'stock' of French investment abroad in 1913 was, it seems, 40 per cent of British 'flows' over the past half century.

Like others, these figures are not wholly free of political manipulation. Yves Guyot, editor of the *Journal des Economistes*, was scoring points in an argument against government 'protectionism'; investment abroad was *not* so great as it was made out to be by such alarmists as the Prime Minister (M. Briand) or the Finance Minister (Raymond Poincaré). Guyot ridiculed the notion that French investors had as much as 5 billion francs (£200 million) in the United States before the war.[4] Then, Lenin forced the figure as high as 60

*Table* 7.1 Existing estimates for French investment abroad before the First World War (£ billions, converted at the current, conventional rate of 25 francs and 5 dollars US to £1 sterling)

| *Source* | *Quantity* | *Date* |
|---|---|---|
| Born | 1.8 | 1914 |
| Crammond | 1.6 | 1909 |
| Feis | 1.8 | 1914 |
| Gille | 1.4/1.6 | 1914 |
| Government (France) | 1.2 | 1901 |
| Guyot | 1.6/1.7 | 1913 |
| Hobson (1) | 1.6 | 1913 |
| Hobson (2) | 1.8 | 1914 |
| League of Nations | 1.7 | 1914 |
| Lenin | 2.4 | 1914 |
| Lévy-Leboyer | 1.7 | 1913 |
| Milward and Saul | 1.6 | 1914 |
| Paish | 1.6 | 1910 |
| Staley | 1.7 | 1914 |
| *The Times* | 1.3 | 1914 |
| United Nations | 1.8 | 1914 |
| White | 1.8 | 1914 |

*Sources*: Several of these estimates, of course, were quoting each other, although often without acknowledgement. They are, *seriatim*: Karl Erich Born, *International Banking in the 19th and 20th Centuries* (Leamington Spa, trans., 1983) p. 122; Edgar Crammond, Paish (1909), discussion p. 483; Herbert Feis, *Europe; the World's Banker* (New Haven, Conn., 1930) p. 47; Bertrand Gille, *Les Investissements Français en Italie, 1815–1914* (Turin, 1968) p. 382; J. A. F. Mackenzie, 'Investments of French Capital Abroad', *Journal of the Royal Statistical Society*, 66 (1903) p. 731 (these were detailed figures by country and occupation gathered and published by the government); Yves Guyot, 'The Amount, Direction and Nature of French Investments', in E. M. Patterson (ed.), *America's Changing Investment Market* (Philadelphia, 1916) p. 43; C. K. Hobson, *The Export of Capital* (1914) p. 69; Ibid., 'British Overseas Investments, Their Growth and Importance', *Annals of the American Academy of Political and Social Science* (1916) p. 32; League of Nations, *The Course and Phases of the World Economic Depression* (Geneva, 1931) p. 28; Lenin, quoted by Maurice Lévy-Leboyer, 'La Capacité Financière de la France au Dêbut du XXe Siècle', in idem. (ed.) *La Position Internationale de la France: Aspects Économiques et Financièrs XIXe–XXe Siècles* (Paris, 1977) p. 9; Lévy-Leboyer, 'La Capacité Financière de la France', p. 9; Alan S. Milward and S. B. Saul, *The Development of the Economies of Continental Europe, 1850–1914* (1977) pp. 492–3; George Paish, 'The Advantage of the Export of Capital by the Older Countries', *Statist*, 1 Jan. 1910, pp. 17–21; Eugene Staley, *War and the Private Investor: A Study in the Relations of International Politics and International Private Investment* (Chicago, 1935) p. 524; 'The French Loan', *The Times*, 29 June 1914, p. 21a; United Nations, *International Capital Movements during the Inter-War Period* (New York, 1949) p. 2; H. D. White, *The French International Accounts, 1880–1913* (Cambridge, Mass., 1933) p. 122.

million francs (£2.4 billion) for France's entire stake in foreign investment in 1914, almost a third as much again as the norm, no doubt to confirm the huge power of metropolitan capitalism.[5]

All the same, even in the knowledge that most of the estimates in Table 7.1 are accumulated aggregates and must be brought down – like Paish's for Britain – to a realistic figure if they are to represent stock, they take account of phenomena more characteristic of French investment than British. It may be that the conventions employed to date for the computation of French investment abroad, generally considered to have been within the range of £1.6 billion to £1.8 billion, have had the effect rather of diminishing the real total than increasing it.

Unlike Britons, Frenchmen invested very heavily through other exchanges, and it is not clear that conventional estimates have taken this fully into account. The French bought many of their US securities through London, Europe's best market. They did the same with 'Kaffirs'. They took up a large part even of London's share in the 'partial' loans of Russia and China. They bought Mexican, Brazilian and Argentine securities through London, and for these and others they made much use of neighbouring bourses in Belgium, Holland, Switzerland, Austria and Germany. For all of these, said Guyot, 'we have no documents allowing us to state a figure'.[6] It may be that such figures can never be established; so much was unrecorded at the time. Bertrand Gille found estimates for France's pre-war investment in Italy that ranged 150 per cent from one billion francs (£40 million) to 2.5 billion (£100 million).[7]

However, the point is that the gap between British and French investment may not have been anything like as large as we have been led to expect. Direct contemporaries understood this very well. Only London and Paris, said the *Economist*, had any big surplus of cash to dispose of, and the two in 1912 were more than ever in command of the world's finance.[8] Yet nearly three years before, the same journal had maintained that the exodus of capital from France was 'almost certainly' *greater* than it was from England.[9] London was still the leading money market of the world, and French bankers were slow to extend mercantile credit (although they were known to hold a great deal of the short-term paper of foreign banks).[10] Margaret Myers was surely right to conclude that French bankers were quite content to see commercial activity financed through London before 1914. But, as she said, 'the only aspect of international finance in which France was then interested was that of investment'.[11]

The question before us is the availability of *new* capital for investment. It is quite possible that even the United States at the turn of the century, and then Germany and later France, had more capital to spare than the United Kingdom. The *Statist*, while it remarked on each episode, found London in 1907 still to be the greatest market both as a clearing house for bills and as a source of new capital.[12] A couple of years later the absolute pre-eminence of London was no longer so clear. Cornelius Rosenraad, President of the Foreign Chambers of Commerce in London, found that Paris by the middle of 1909 had become the principal market for international securities.[13] Viscount Milner, addressing an audience of Midland businessmen in October 1913, thought that it was really only in Great Britain and France – 'perhaps above all in France' – that any considerable amount of surplus capital might be placed at the disposal of other nations.[14]

Such ideas were commonly held at the time, and they were true. Paris, although more affected by the capital 'famine' and alarms of the Balkan Wars, had ceased to be 'second only' to London.[15] For the moment, said the *Economist* in January 1914, London was no longer the centre of the capital market; borrowers turned not to London but to Paris.[16] Yves Guyot, looking back on the years immediately before the war, was sure that because Britain was so overcommitted at home and abroad, not least in defence, France had the larger amount of latent capital awaiting its opportunity abroad. Paris even now was not the foremost banker in the world, nor did Frenchmen own as much capital, at home and abroad, as Great Britain or even the United States. But France was the country where most new capital was available.[17]

Even if we must allow for the rhetoric of a politician, Raymond Poincaré was not entirely misleading when he apostrophised France as an 'indefatigable creator of wealth'; France works, she produces, she economises, and that is why her market is always the biggest reservoir of capital in the world'.[18]

## GERMANY AS AN INVESTOR ABROAD IN AUGUST 1914

The figures for Germany are even less reliable. As recently as the late 1970s, Karl Born could find no precise data for the volume of

Germany's capital exports before 1914; on the whole, he himself preferred a compromise between two Feis estimates,[19] both published as far back as 1930. Better figures must surely be available by now; meanwhile, a selection of some of the more frequently cited is given in Table 7.2 below.

*Table* 7.2 Existing estimates for German investment abroad before the First World War (£ billions, converted at the current, conventional rate of 12 marks and 5 dollars US to £1 sterling)

| *Source* | *Quantity* | *Date* |
|---|---|---|
| Born | 1.12 | 1913 |
| Crammond | 1.5 | 1909–10 |
| Feis | 1.05–1.2 | 1913 |
| Hobson | 1.0 | 1914 |
| League of Nations | 1.1 | 1914 |
| Milward and Saul | 1.2 | 1914 |
| Paish | 1.6 | 1909–10 |
| Rosenraad | 1.6 | 1909 |
| United Nations | 1.2 | 1914 |

*Sources*: Karl Erich Born, *International Banking in the 19th and 20th Centuries* (Leamington Spa, trans., 1983) p. 133; Edgar Crammond, Paish (1909), discussion p. 483, and 'The Economic Position of Germany', *Quarterly Review* (April 1910) p. 488; Herbert Feis, *Europe, the World's Banker* (New Haven, Conn., 1930) p. 71; C. K. Hobson, 'British Overseas Investments, Their Growth and Importance', *Annals of the American Academy of Political and Social Science* (Philadelphia, 1916) p. 32; League of Nations, *The Course and Phases of the World Economic Depression* (Geneva, 1931) p. 28; Alan S. Milward and S. B. Saul, *The Development of the Economies of Continental Europe, 1850–1914* (1977) p. 493; George Paish (1909), discussion p. 495 and 'The Advantage of the Export of Capital by the Older Countries', *Statist*, 1, Jan. 1910, pp. 17–21; Cornelius Rosenraad, Paish (1909), discussion p. 491; United Nations, *International Capital Movements during the Inter-War Period* (New York, 1949) p. 2.

Like the totals for French foreign investment (Table 7.1 above), much confusion exists between 'stock' and 'flows'. There is a hint of national hysteria, shown particularly in the Crammond and Paish numbers for 1909–10 when the threat of German competition was very much at the back of every mind. Above all, uncertain account (if any) has been taken of Germany's large holdings of stocks and shares in other markets. Germans bought a great deal in London – the securities of the United States, of Canada, South Africa, Brazil and Spanish America amongst others – and had done so for years.

Whereas Britons cared little for Central and Eastern Europe before the excitement of Rumanian oil, Germany was deeply engaged. Bernard Michel calculates that about a third of Germany's investment abroad by 1916 was in Austria–Hungary, an area in which Britain had shown a 'singulier manque d'intérêt'.[20] When the Hungarian Government issued a large quantity of Crown *rentes* in January 1911, 64 per cent of the vast subscription came from Germany.[21] Germans, like Frenchmen 'under the stress of high taxation and stringent bourse regulations', bought heavily in Continental markets like Brussels so that it became impracticable in the years before the war to distinguish Belgian ownership from what belonged to Germans and French.[22]

It may never be possible to assemble the elements, although one might doubt C. K. Hobson's deduction that Germany's investment abroad just before the war 'did not perhaps greatly exceed £1 000 000 000'.[23] If I am right in reducing Britain's total of portfolio investment to £2.6 billion while suggesting simultaneously that both France and Germany had more invested abroad in 1914, portfolio and direct, than had previously been estimated, some of the usual explanations and conclusions may have to be altered. In the meantime, however, hard figures do not exist.

## FINAL CONCLUSIONS

Sir Alexander Cairncross found that all estimates for the stock of Britain's holdings abroad before 1914 were 'necessarily extremely rough . . . mere guesswork [which was] at one point or another quite unavoidable'.[24] This was true enough for such figures as existed before the First World War, as it was for British official statistics even after the Second.[25] Quantitative data, although always attractive to the economic historian, are not inviolate; too large a conclusion can easily be drawn. Surely it can no longer be said, with Herbert Feis, that Britain's ownership of securities abroad was about £4 billion by 1914, well over a quarter of Britain's national wealth.[26]

Guesswork is indeed inescapable, although some guesses are preferable to others. A long technical essay, said Feis, might be written on the accurate measurement of Britain's foreign investment.

This does not, of course, prevent us from trying, any more than it did Feis himself. But at least it encourages a proper humility.

Portfolio investment was the 'most important single item' within the total of British investment overseas before 1914, for which George Paish, Keynes said, had supplied extremely valuable material *towards* making an estimate. But there were other important elements undisclosed, and Keynes thought that Paish, in 1911, had not furnished 'even a temporary estimate of foreign investments proper'.[27]

A more realistic account of 'direct' investment would help. It is said that British capital exporters were uninterested in manufacturing, and this would appear to be the case if portfolio investment were so overwhelmingly large in proportion to direct investment before 1914; it would not be so if that ratio were disturbed. Dunning maintains that 90 per cent of all international capital investments in 1914 took the form of portfolio investment even within a modern and more comprehensive definition of 'direct'.[28] But it may be that conditions after the war were not changed quite so radically as all that, and that Mira Wilkins was right in suggesting that direct investment was more significant than has generally been supposed.[29] In any case, far less money may have been available for new investment than anybody has thought, either at the time or since. It was discovered, for example, in the early summer of 1907 that not even a favourite like the 5 per cent loan at 97 guaranteed by the Japanese Government could be floated without help from the underwriters.[30]

We have grown accustomed to huge international debts and to their consequences; but as W. Arthur Lewis reminds us, a big change took place during and after the First World War. The limited budgets of tropical countries from 1880 to 1913 reflected the ability of their governments to manage on taxes representing as little as 4 to 5 per cent of the national income, while modern industrial nations themselves in 1913 took only 8 to 10 per cent.[31] Quite high rates of growth, say Alan Green and M. C. Urquhart, can be supported from domestic saving; Germany was self-sufficient throughout, the United States very nearly so after the Civil War and certainly from 1890, Italy from the 1890s.[32] The same applied to most of the countries with which I myself have worked both before and after 1870.[33] Fewer foreign securities were held in 1914 because less foreign investment was wanted.

Such doubts are legion, and I have suggested only a few of the directions in which estimates and conclusions may be expected to change. One target in this book is the ready acceptance of an important number, followed by its misapplication to reach what must become misleading conclusions. In practice, it is only from a satisfactory base that econometric games can be played. In the words of the Chinese proverb: 'When you drink of the water, remember the spring.'

## Notes

1. Alexander Dana Moyes, *Financial Chapters of the War* (1916) pp. 78, 82, 203; he repeats the argument in *The War Period of American Finance, 1908–1925* (New York, 1926) p. 127.
2. Maurice Lévy-Leboyer, 'La Capacité Financière de la France au Début du XXe Siècle', in idem (ed.), *La Position Internationale de la France: Aspects Économiques et Financiers XIXe–XXe Siècles* (Paris, 1977) p. 9.
3. Ibid. p. 32.
4. Y. Guyot, 'The Amount, Direction and Nature of French Investments', in E. M. Patterson (ed.), *America's Changing Investment Market* (Philadelphia, 1916) pp. 43, 52.
5. As quoted by Lévy-Leboyer, 'La Capacité Financière de la France', p. 9.
6. Guyot, 'Amount, Direction and Nature of French Investments', p. 52.
7. B. Gille, *Les Investissements Français en Italie, 1815–1914* (Turin, 1968) p. 382.
8. 'Nine Months New Capital', *Economist*, 5 Oct. 1912, p. 610.
9. *Economist*, 1 Jan. 1910, p. 6.
10. B. M. Anderson, *Effects of the War on Money, Credit and Banking in France and the United States* (New York, 1919) pp. 41–2.
11. M. Myers, *Paris as a Financial Centre* (1936) p. 1. She does not, however, take account of short-term credits by French branch banks in London.
12. 'Our Exports of Capital – England Resumes Her Position', *Statist*, 20 July 1907, p. 101.
13. Paish (1909), discussion p. 485.
14. Milner, 'The Scramble for Capital', *Journal of the Institute of Bankers*, 34 (Dec. 1913) p. 612. He was giving a presidential address to the Birmingham and Midland Institute.
15. As, for example, in Marcello de Cecco, *Money and Empire: The International Gold Standard, 1890–1914* (Oxford, 1974) p. 106.
16. 'A Year's Capital Issues', *Economist*, 3 Jan. 1914, p. 8.

17. Guyot, 'Amount, Direction and Nature of French Investments', p. 54.
18. Ibid., p. 36.
19. K. Born, *International Banking in the 19th and 20th Centuries* (first published in Stuttgart 1977 and republished in translation at Leamington Spa, 1983) p. 133.
20. B. Michel, *Banques et Banquiers en Autriche au Début du 20*e *Siècle* (Paris, 1976) pp. 242, 255.
21. *Economist*, 14 Jan. 1911, p. 61.
22. J. A. Hobson, *An Economic Interpretation of Investment* (n.d., but probably 1911) p. 76.
23. C. K. Hobson, 'British Overseas Investments, Their Growth and Importance', *Annals of the American Academy of Political and Social Science* (Philadelphia, 1916) p. 32.
24. Sir Alexander Cairncross, *Home and Foreign Investment, 1870–1913: Studies in Capital Accumulation* (Cambridge, 1953) p. 182.
25. See Peter Clarke's review of Cairncross's most recent book, *Years of Recovery: British Economic Policy 1945–51* (1985), published in the *Times Literary Supplement*, 21 June 1985, p. 683.
26. H. Feis, *Europe, the World's Banker 1870–1914* (New Haven, Conn., 1930) p. 15.
27. Paish (1911), discussion p. 195.
28. John H. Dunning, *Studies in International Investment* (1970) pp. 2–3.
29. M. Wilkins, 'Modern European Economic History and the Multinationals', *Journal of European Economic History*, 6, 3 (Winter, 1977) p. 591 – although the reference is to the wider definition of 'direct' investment now current.
30. 'Why Are Consols So Low?', *Investors' Monthly Manual* (July 1907) p. 385.
31. W. A. Lewis (ed.), *Tropical Development 1880–1913: Studies in Economic Progress* (1970) p. 36.
32. A. Green and M. C. Urquhart, 'Factor and Commodity Flows in the International Economy of 1870–1914: A Multi Country View', *Journal of Economic History*, 36 (1976) pp. 246–7.
33. D. C. M. Platt, *Foreign Finance in Continental Europe and the United States, 1815–1870* (1984), and in articles that take the story to 1914, including 'Dependency in Nineteenth Century Latin America: An Historian Objects', *Latin American Research Review*, 15 (1980) pp. 113–30, and 'Financing the Expansion of Cities, 1860–1914', *Urban History Review*, XI (1983) pp. 61–6.

# Appendix 1 The Underwriting of Loans on the London Stock Exchange

I referred in Chapter 2 – under 'amortisations, repayments, defaults and losses' – to the practice of 'underwriting' on the London Exchange. The outcome of underwriting is more relevant to 'flow' estimates than it is to 'stock'. Yet the great increase in underwriting during the pre-war years led to problems for any stock estimate that is based on Paish. It should be said from the outset that the understanding, in Paish and others, that an underwritten loan was *ipso facto* fully subscribed is inaccurate.

Underwriters, in return for a commission, undertook to take back the unsold portion of a loan. Normally the system worked smoothly enough. Most public issues were underwritten in the years leading up to the First World War and, ideally, the whole of the unsold portion either returned and was sold ultimately to the market, or passed more permanently into the portfolio of insurance or trust companies (themselves often active as underwriters of new issues). Underwriters who took back unsold securities were entitled in any case to their commission; they could unload when the market improved, or sell immediately at less than the original price. It was a good business if the market held. Loans that returned to the underwriters were not necessarily failures; there is evidence that genuine investors before the war were deliberately holding back their subscriptions until after allotment to buy later from the underwriters at a discount.[1] Eighteen per cent of a government of Canada loan of June 1914 was taken back by the underwriters; later the same day (*The Times* reported) there was 'some steady buying by investors who had waited for the closing of the lists'.[2]

All the same, there is evidence of extreme pressure on underwriters, and many issues remained unsold. The history of underwritten loans was alarming, and an indication of the percentage of major loans left with the underwriters is shown in Table A.1 below.

It is possible to maintain that these issues were unloaded eventually on the investor. If that were the case, the fact of an underwriting 'failure' would make little difference to Britain's 'stock' of investment, since the loans remained as liabilities to the borrower whether held still by the underwriters or spread more widely among genuine investors. The *Economist* warned that its figures for new capital applications, from 1907 to 1911 inclusive, might exaggerate the sum actually bought for investment since they were compiled from the securities *offered*, and in some cases the amounts *taken* were far less; yet nearly every important issue was underwritten, and 'therefore the whole of it finds its way ultimately either on to the market or into the hands of an insurance or trust company'.[3]

*Table* A.1 Issues left with their underwriters, 1908–14

| *Description* | *Year* | *Amount* (£ million) | *Percentage left with underwriter* |
|---|---|---|---|
| New South Wales | 1908 | 3.0 | 90 |
| B.A. Great Southern | 1908 | 2.0 | 40 |
| Salvador | 1908 | 1.0 | 'nearly whole' |
| Grand Trunk Rly (Canada) | 1908 | 2.0 | 90 |
| Southern Nigeria | 1908 | 3.0 | 95 |
| Montreal | 1908 | 1.0 | 65 |
| East India Rly | 1908 | 2.45 | 90 |
| Sweden | 1908 | 3.0 | 97 |
| Burma Rlys | 1908 | 1.0 | 75 |
| Canada (October issue) | 1908 | 5.0 | 75 |
| Bombay Baroda Rly | 1908 | 1.0 | 75 |
| Oceanic Steam Navigation Co. | 1908 | 1.25 | 50 |
| Midland Rly (Uruguay) | 1908 | 0.6 | 90 |
| Saskatchewan | 1908 | 0.4 | 75 |
| Canada | 1909 | 6.5 | 49 |
| New South Wales | 1909 | 3.0 | 50/60 |
| Anglo-Argentine Tramways | 1909 | 3.5 | 70 |
| Grand Trunk Rly | 1909 | 1.0 | 77 |
| Gothenburg | 1909 | 0.9 | 85 |
| Lake Superior Corp. (Canada) | 1909 | 1.0 | 90 |
| Port of Calcutta | 1909 | 0.7 | 83 |
| Colombia Navigation | 1909 | 0.45 | 97½ |
| Turkey | 1909 | 2.0 | 80 |
| Ceylon | 1909 | 1.5 | 'large amount' |
| Montenegro | 1909 | 0.25 | 90 |
| Straits Settlements | 1910 | 2.8 | 93 |
| New Zealand | 1910 | 5.0 | 92 |
| Grand Trunk Pacific Rly (Canada) | 1910 | 1.0 | 50 |
| Budapest | 1910 | 2.0 | 'most of it' |
| Canada | 1910 | 5.0 | 78 |
| Persia | 1911 | 1.3 | 'largely' |
| Northern Ontario | 1911 | 7.0 | 90 |
| Greece | 1911 | 0.8 | 90 |
| Tokyo | 1912 | 3.2 | 50 |
| Moscow | 1912 | 3.8 | 45 |
| Rio de Janeiro (State) | 1912 | 3.0 | 83 |
| Anglo-French Mercantile Co. | 1912 | 0.6 | 90 |
| India | 1912 | 3.0 | 85 |
| Canada | 1912 | 5.0 | 50 |
| West Australia | 1912 | 1.0 | 50 |
| Canada | 1913 | 3.0 | 56 |
| Victoria (Canada) | 1913 | 2.0 | 53 |
| West Australia | 1913 | 1.0 | 72 |

| *Description* | *Year* | *Amount* (£ million) | *Percentage left with underwriter* |
|---|---|---|---|
| Vancouver Power | 1913 | 0.7 | 86 |
| New South Wales | 1914 | 3.0 | 80 |
| Budapest | 1914 | 1.0 | 80 |
| Montreal | 1914 | 1.5 | 37 |
| Russian Govt Rly | 1914 | 3.1 | 75 |
| South Africa | 1914 | 4.0 | 65 |
| Greater Winnipeg Water | 1914 | 0.4 | 97 |
| South Africa | 1914 | 4.0 | 80 |
| Córdoba Central Rly (Argentina) | 1914 | 1.3 | 80 |
| Canada (Govt, March) | 1914 | 5.0 | 78 |
| Grand Trunk Rly | 1914 | 1.5 | 53 |
| British Columbia | 1914 | 1.5 | 50 |
| Canada (Govt, June) | 1914 | 5.0 | 88 |
| Kieff | 1914 | 2.1 | 96 |
| St Petersburg | 1914 | 2.3 | 88 |
| Ontario | 1914 | 1.0 | 90 |
| Northern Rly (Canada) | 1914 | 3.0 | 79 |

*Source*: *The Times*, 'City Intelligence' and *Economist* (Investors' Monthly Manual). The list is not comprehensive, and percentages returned to underwriters were not always common to sources although within the same range. National, Provincial and City names indicate public issues (e.g. 'Canada' for the Dominion, 'Saskatchewan' for the Province and 'Montreal' for the city).

This was generally the case. Hartley Withers, editor of the *Economist*, was confident that most underwriters of his own generation took full responsibility. A Colonial loan, he said, might not go off well because of 'some accident in the monetary atmosphere', but the underwriters, finding themselves saddled with unsold securities, could easily borrow on them (as trustee securities) and, in better times, unload them again on trustees or other real investors. By contrast, an issue of some minor European power or of a Latin American republic, coldly received by the investing public (and not saleable to trustees), was expensive from the beginning in underwriting charges and might be left with the underwriters for years before being sold at a discount.[4]

My intention, however, is to suggest a stock figure, and the point to watch is the history of what happened to the securities once withdrawn by the underwriters. First, were they unloaded on the *British* investor, thus becoming part of the stock of *British* investment overseas, or did they find a market elsewhere? Second, was underwriting always genuine, or did some of it, although required for marketing a new issue, mean nothing at all?

Underwriting was a natural development from a practice common to international markets since Waterloo – the syndication of issues among financiers, taken 'firm'. It was respectable and familiar at first, but standards had fallen, and they fell for decades. A leading article in the *Economist* of 1890 warned readers of the swarm of new companies, 'trusts, debenture corporations, trustees and insurance corporations', that was busying itself in underwriting securities and then unloading them by degrees on the general public.[5] Twenty years later, the *Economist* restated the principle that the underwriter agreed to take up any stock or shares he might underwrite, but it confirmed that considerable changes were taking place in the market, that underwriting no longer always meant what it was supposed to mean, and that there was substantial evasion.[6]

By the late 1900s, underwriters included jobbers on the Stock Exchange, banks, discount houses, trust companies, joint stock syndicates and minor financial houses. Their function was to create an illusion of security among possible investors and to 'puff' the new stock to a premium. Their transactions were then recorded in the 'money articles' of the newspapers, 'and in this way the public is induced to believe that there is a great demand for the new issue'.[7] Hartley Withers quoted 1 to 3 per cent as the price of underwriting on big national loans backed by good houses. Private undertakings, except for the great railways, were seldom fathered by a leading financial firm, and industrial ventures were left to smaller fry in search of a high commission. Withers described an imaginary industrial security, the Hygienic Tooth-Powder Company Ltd. It was underwritten at 10 per cent, and had incurred further expenses for general promotion, advertising (direct and indirect), repurchases of shares to support the market, 'names' on the Board, testimonials, cash to dealers and newspapers, so that a great gulf opened between the paper purchase price and the sum that actually reached the borrower.[8]

Much of this was bad luck for the borrower; the liability remained whatever was lost in between. The 'stock' figure remained intact. Some years were better than others. Underwriters were left with much on their hands at the beginning of this century. They recovered during the upsurge on security markets from the summer of 1904, but after the financial crisis of 1907 (mainly in the United States), they were left with a major part of new loans in 1908 and their digestion was reported as 'rather overworked' by the summer of 1909. The first half of 1910 was no better, after which the market much improved until the early summer of 1912 when several recent issues were once more reported as 'thrown largely upon the underwriters'. There was a short respite during the second half of 1912, but fears of war in the Balkans and elsewhere kept the market in a fright throughout 1913; Thomas Skinner, editor of the *Stock Exchange Year Book*, reported that underwriters even of first class securities had in many cases been compelled to take back very large blocks 'ranging from 50 to 90 per cent of the total offered',[9] and the same was reported by the *Banker's Magazine*.[10] Underwriters in the City, in December 1913, were 'being compelled to carry securities of the very best class to an extent becoming intolerable'.[11] Early in 1914 the underwriters were back in action, only to vanish once more as political insecurity destroyed the market for spring and early summer to August 1914.

Contemporary views of the quality and reality of underwriting are very uncertain, but the problems it raises cannot be dismissed altogether. The hints of evasion, even of fraud, are too pervasive, and they had been so since the early 1890s. The underwriters of the failed Victoria (Australia) Loan of 1902 (£1 million) were 'relieved of their guarantees'.[12] An issue could be 'totally or partially withdrawn by the responsible financial institution'.[13] The *Financial Times* made a distinction between underwriting accepted by a firm and by a limited liability syndicate: 'There [was] always some hold on the former if of recognised status, but the latter may be a thing of straw . . . By voluntarily winding up [it] would vanish into oblivion, as numbers have already done.'[14] It did not follow that securities unsold in London were held by Britons. Foreign and Imperial branch banks were well represented among London underwriters, and when their guarantees were called in it was not British capital, necessarily, that took the burden. The international character of the London market made it possible even for British underwriters, and more so for foreigners, to unload loans abroad that had failed to sell in London. Paish reported £1.8 million of London 'subscriptions' for Egypt in 1908, when in reality the underwriters had been compelled to take back 80 per cent of the £1.5 million issued by the Agricultural Bank of Egypt, and the bonds had been sold immediately at a discount on the Continent.[15] The practice was not unusual, even when it did not reflect the outcome of failed issues and their underwriters. Statements were reported in the Canadian press, early in 1909, to the effect that the Canadian Pacific Railway had recently made a private sale of nearly 40 000 shares accumulated from issues in which holders had not taken up the full proportion for which they had subscribed; part of this block had been taken in Germany.[16]

Quality counted, and it was this that was often lacking in the practice of underwriting before 1914. Hartley Withers told his readers in 1910 that during the current boom in the securities of rubber plantations 'many people had made money out of underwriting when they could not have honoured their promises'.[17] I can offer no figures. The extent of failure was often unknown, and sometimes deliberately concealed. One million pounds in Grand Trunk Pacific Railway debentures were claimed as 'successfully placed' in February 1909; three days later it was reported that the underwriters had actually been left with about 77 per cent.[18] A Southern Nigeria Loan of £5 million was launched in London in the autumn of 1911. Consols fell on the news of underwriting, and rose again when it was heard that the loan was a success; they declined when it was discovered that the loan had not been as well received as it had been said to be and was only just covered by subscriptions.[19] All that can be said – in the maze of contradictions – is that the problem existed and should be taken into account.

**Notes**

1. 'New Issues and the Investor', *Economist*, 20 Dec. 1913, p. 1340; 'Poor Response to Capital Issues', *The Times*, 15 July 1914, 21b.
2. *The Times*, 12 June 1914, p. 21c.
3. 'The Year's New Capital', *Economist*, 30 Dec. 1911, p. 1357.
4. H. Withers, *International Finance* (1916) pp. 147–8.
5. *Economist*, 26 April 1890, pp. 517–18.
6. Ibid. 3 June 1911, pp. 1183–4.
7. Henry Lowenfeld, *All About Investment* (1909) p. 173.
8. Withers, *Stocks and Shares* (London, 1917) p. 71.
9. Skinner's preface, dated November 1913, to *The Stock Exchange Yearbook for 1914* (1914) p. vi.
10. *Banker's Magazine* (Nov. 1913) p. 580.
11. *Investors' Review*, 27 December 1913, p. 864.
12. 'Colonial Borrowing', *Economist*, 26 July 1902, p. 1166.
13. Matthew Simon, 'The Pattern of New British Portfolio Foreign Investment 1865–1914', in J. H. Adler (ed.), *Capital Markets and Economic Development* (New York, 1967) p. 36.
14. Financial Times, *Investors' Guide* (1913) p. 45.
15. *The Times*, 14 May 1908, p. 15b.
16. Ibid., 5 March 1909, p. 18c.
17. Withers, 'Underwriters and Subscribers', *Investors' Monthly Manual* (Oct. 1910) p. 586.
18. *The Times*, 24 Feb. 1909, 21b, and ibid., 27 Feb. 1909, 15a.
19. *Investors' Monthly Manual* (Nov. 1911) p. 639.

# Appendix 2 The 'Income Tax Method' for the Computation of Britain's Overseas Investment

Amongst the relatively meagre information available for computing the extent of British investment overseas, Sir George Paish found 'one set of information of great value – the incomes assessed to income tax'.[1] Paish was following in the footsteps of his former associate and senior, Sir Robert Giffen, for whom the use of income tax returns as a measure of Britain's overseas investment (and much else besides) had become something of a personal 'corner' – so much so that it came to be known as the 'Giffen method' although he was not himself its inventor. Sir Josiah Stamp has since suggested many of its disadvantages as a method, which include a limit for exemption from tax that was rather higher for Britain than for other countries (so that some part of the income was not in fact recorded), the liability to error that arose from the different approaches to the basis of capitalisation, and the evasion of tax. But Stamp concluded, with whatever reservations, that 'on the whole the estimate of income [from income tax returns] having regard to the nature of the data and the methods employed is perhaps the most accurate available for any country, and is certainly in Grade I'.[2]

Within the broad computation of national wealth in which Sir Josiah was currently engaged, he may have been right; for the more focused identification of Britain's stock of investment abroad, the deficiencies of the 'income tax method' become more obvious. Sir Robert Giffen was a statistician of great contemporary repute; anything he set his hand to, said the *Economist* in 1904, 'can hardly be given a higher character'.[3] Sir George Paish, joint editor of one of London's most powerful financial weeklies, the *Statist*, was knighted for his services even before he became special financial adviser to the Chancellor of the Exchequer. Is it possible that these two knights of the *Belle Époque* have lent authority to a set of methods and conclusions that might otherwise have escaped notice?

Sir George Paish's estimates caught the public eye at a time of particularly energetic debate between Liberal Free Traders and Conservative tariff reformers. It was the 'income tax method' that seemingly authenticated both Sir Robert Giffen's estimates and those of Sir George. Paish, in the first part of his 1909 paper, used the income tax returns for 1907–8 (together with his own compilation of company income for 1907) to arrive at a figure for total income received from foreign securities. This he compared with his aggregated, annual totals of public and private securities (portfolio), calculating the interest on the whole to be just over 5 per cent. It was an odd procedure, since he was relating a figure for income on the stock of investment (at various points from 1906 to 1908) to an accumulated total of British investment that went back well into the previous century. But the 'method', superficially, seemed authentic. If income tax returns (on interest received from foreign securities) were capable of producing accurate information on quantity and distribution, what remained in dispute?

## INCOME RECORDED BY THE COMMISSIONERS OF INLAND REVENUE

Serious problems existed with the kind of data available to the Commissioners before the war, most of which were acknowledged quite openly at the time; the returns must be regarded, said Edgar Crammond, as 'so deficient in many material particulars that they are quite untrustworthy for the purpose of giving a comprehensive idea as to the total of [Britain's overseas] investments or of the income earned'.[4] Crammond was too dismissive, but the Commissioners themselves explained why their figures should be regarded as of limited value. It was important to bear in mind, they said, that the information at their disposal indicated only the income identified for the purpose of taxation; their tables were 'necessarily different from figures of total receipts from overseas, whether profits or not, which are the figures of direct importance for the purpose of the international balance of payments.'[5]

Over the years the quality and coverage improved. The Commissioners first took serious account of the problem after 1870. In a useful report on tax administration for the previous fourteen years (1856 to 1869), they found that income tax returns were 'largely deficient' in every degree; 40 per cent of the persons assessed had understated their incomes to such an extent that genuine returns would imply an addition of 130 per cent. One estimate cited by the Commissioners indicated that on income tax overall, duty had been evaded on 56.6 per cent of the income that should have been returned; they had no cause to distrust this estimate, and at all events, no reason to find it excessive.[6]

C. K. Hobson derived his figures from the improved estimates available after 1870. He took the full range of tax receipts on overseas investment from the early 1870s to the tax year 1913–14, and set it off against Paish's calculation of unassessed income for the single year 1907. This procedure is mentioned in my discussion of methods in Part I, where I refer to Imlah's decision also to use the same unlikely projection – with the difference that Imlah started from the tax year 1886–7 (by which time the coverage had greatly improved, since Section 26 of the Customs and Inland Revenue Act of 1885 provided for the direct deduction and payment by bankers and dealers in Britain of income tax in respect of interest and dividends on foreign and colonial investments).

The Commissioners explained in each of their Annual Reports that their knowledge of income from abroad 'so far as [that income] can be identified' was taken solely from the returns of appointed agents of foreign and colonial governments and companies for the payment of interest in Britain, from bankers and coupon dealers for both governments and companies, and from British companies with a seat in Britain that owned and worked railways abroad. These declared an income of £118 million in the tax year 1913–14, but the Commissioners found that 'beyond this earmarked figure there exists a large amount of income from abroad which in many cases cannot (in the absence of details which the taxpayer alone could furnish) be identified as such in the assessment'.[7]

For all their limitations, tax returns have been found convenient because they seem at least to indicate a minimum of investment within an important range of securities. They attract because they appear to offer 'hard evidence' where so little exists elsewhere. Tax figures were employed as weapons in the debate between tariff reformers and Free Traders, between Conservatives and Liberals; at issue was the supposedly high rate of tax evasion induced by Lloyd George's tax reforms, and the extent to which Liberal taxation on land and income was driving 'Loyd George investments' overseas rather than releasing it for productive employment at home.[8]

Sir Felix Schuster, once an additional Income Tax Commissioner for the City of London, was sure that tax returns on the whole were straightforward and honest so long as the taxpayer understood what he was supposed to do; the flagrant cases were very few.[9] Schuster was answering the accusations of that controversial figure Pethick Lawrence, who was currently (1919) promoting the idea of a capital levy; to some degree his ideas were prejudiced by his politics, as were those of J. M. Keynes when he argued, as a Liberal Free Trader in 1910, that tax evasion was 'immensely exaggerated' by Conservative tariff reformers. But Keynes made the legitimate point that it was far easier for foreigners to evade tax in Britain than it was for Britons with their securities abroad: 'A would-be evader [in Britain] must first choose very carefully a *special class* of foreign investment, must then take precautions for remittance to this country through other than the usual channels, and must finally fill up a false declaration.'[10] And it was true that ever since the Inland Revenue Act of 1885 it had become difficult to escape income tax in full within Britain, since tax was deducted on the coupons of government stocks and of certain classes of public companies before it ever reached the investors.[11]

Avner Offer quotes an Inland Revenue report of January 1914 to the effect that a recent survey of the hundred largest payers of surtax in Britain and a scrutiny of death duty accounts had failed to identify more than a handful of cases where declared income had fallen since Lloyd George's budget proposals of 1909, although some of the exceptions, like the Duke of Westminster and Viscount Iveagh were important . . .[12] Kennedy's recent research among Scottish probates suggests that there is no evidence of systematic tax evasion, while he himself has formed the 'distinct impression' from probate on British estates generally (English and Scottish) that tax avoidance, in those years of low rates before 1914, was considered more onerous than payment.[13]

Deliberate evasion was not, then, a cause of serious distortion in the tax figures; they did not understate British revenue from foreign investment on this account. What they did, however, within their limited coverage, was rather to conceal the real extent of foreign ownership of securities through London. Income tax from 1905 to 1909 was levied at the rate of 5 per cent (one shilling in the pound). It was raised by a further 1 per cent in 1909, when a surtax of 2½ per cent was added for incomes over £5000. Surtax was unlikely to affect any but the very largest of holdings, domestic or foreign, and a low general rate was not decisive in compelling investors resident abroad to identify themselves in return for the minimal tax exemption to which they were entitled. The figures for exemption in the reports of the Commissioners are not helpful; they record payments only through agents in the UK, for which application had to be made within six months of the end of the financial year. As a contemporary tax guide explained, 'the small investor, in many cases, did not consider it worthwhile to go to the trouble of making a claim for the recovery of tax from his dividend and interest warrants', and may not even have been aware that he could do so.[14] Paish claimed too much when he told his critics in 1911 that they might 'rest assured that the [foreign] Government loans on which income tax was paid [in Britain] were British capital'.[15]

The great attraction of London to foreigners was the vastly wider range of securities on sale. But the British tax system was also often an advantage. In London, where companies were registered under laws other than those of England and Scotland, non-residents could arrange for British tax not to be deducted. Bonds or bearer shares on which coupons were payable outside London, or where the register of stockholders was kept abroad, were not recorded at all on British tax returns. The critical difference was between companies registered in London and those registered abroad. British registered companies had income tax deducted from dividend and interest payments, and it could not be recovered. All companies registered under foreign laws (including those of the British Empire) had coupons payable in places other than Britain, and if interest were paid in London it was repayable. The Buenos Aires and Pacific Railway Company, for example, was registered under English law, with its bond interest payable only in London, while the Buenos Aires Central was registered under Argentine law and its coupons could be paid not only in London, but also in Buenos Aires and New York. A non-British investor in companies registered under the laws of British Dominions, Colonies or foreign countries, having bought his shares in London, had merely to ask for his holding to be registered abroad to secure that his dividends were remitted to him from head office without deduction of British income tax. This, as Emil Davies explains, was the case with South African mining companies, most of which were registered under South African law; although sold through London, their chief market was on the Continent, and their head offices were in Johannesburg.[16] Ownership of bearer securities, increasingly common at the time, was unidentifiable; holders resident outside the United Kingdom, if they took the trouble, could obtain payment through London without deduction of British income tax.

In some of these cases the suggestion must be that *rather more* foreign-owned securities were held in London than has normally been thought to be the case, even within the limited compass of deductions from British income tax. British tax lists took no account of what was certainly the case up to the 1930s: the registration of securities with British banks as nominees, or even with individuals, that were really the property of foreigners.[17] For a number of reasons, the quantities could be quite large. Whatever the outcome, it cannot be said that the annual reports of the Commissioners before 1914 are a conclusive source of evidence, while the random and spasmodic survival of British taxation papers in the Public Record Office gives no further guidance. The distance is still great between 1914 and the end of the 1920s, when Sir Robert Kindersley was able to say with some confidence that at least within the area of outstanding sterling loans of English and foreign governments and municipalities, foreign holdings could 'roughly [be] indicated by the amount of interest paid in London free of income tax'.[18]

## BALANCE OF INCOME UNRECORDED FOR TAX

Figures from the Inland Revenue have at least the merit of consistency; furthermore, they bear the official imprimatur. Estimates for the remaining portion, the 'large amount which cannot be identified in the assessments', are far more open to doubt.

One of those useful conventions that develop over the years is the notion that the unidentified portion in Britain's revenue from overseas investment was about equal in size to the part that appeared in the reports of the Commissioners. Sir Robert Giffen, when he first considered the point for the tax year 1875, found that the sum total of the Inland Revenue Commissioners for income derived from the investment of British capital abroad was £29 million, while his own estimate, incorporating the unidentified revenue, came to as much as £65 million; no less than £40 million (as he said later) should be taken as the income from abroad omitted from the income tax returns.[19] In 1906, the *Financial Review of Reviews* and the *Economist* both agreed on a division of about half and half.[20] Sir George Paish took the £82.8 million compiled by the Commissioners for 1907–8 and added a further £58 million for dividends undisclosed (41 per cent).[21] Edgar Crammond, for the tax year 1908–9, settled for 48 per cent: £88.8 million compiled by the Commissioners and a further £81.2 million for revenues undisclosed.[22] The *Board of Trade Journal* quoted the Commissioners' figure of £118 million for the financial year 1913–14, and then brought it up to 'no less than £210 000 000'.[23]

It is quite impossible to be precise. Sir Robert Giffen had allowed a further 62 per cent; Sir George Paish, with uncharacteristic restraint, put it at 41 per cent; Crammond thought that it might be 48 per cent; the Board of Trade brought it back up to 44 per cent. Within this range some figure must surely have been right, and the 50/50 of the financial reviews is no doubt a sensible compromise. The trouble begins when too much is expected from a total figure for Britain's revenue from investment overseas which contains both a weak component for income tax received, and barely more than a guess for income on dividends that are not recorded. If the result is capitalised at the formula of twenty years' purchase, itself randomly selected, the figure is likely to contain some spectacular errors. Twenty years' purchase is certainly the convention, but Paul Arndt is not alone in wondering whether the simple multiplication of an income figure by twenty produces a very likely result for stock.[24]

The point is worth pursuing. Sir Josiah Stamp has mentioned the liability to error that arises from so many different approaches to capitalisation – that is, to the appropriate number of years' revenue 'purchase' to be allowed in assessing full capital value.[25] The differences are wide indeed. Giffen had presented his formulae back in 1889. They varied from twenty-eight years' purchase on UK railways, to only four years for 'quarries, mines, ironworks and gasworks'. As for foreign investments, Giffen allocated twenty years' purchase to those covered by Inland Revenue assessment (foreign and colonial governments and municipalities in Schedule C, and railways out of the United Kingdom in Schedule D); but he capitalised foreign dividends that were not incorporated at ten years' purchase.[26]

Paish used capitalisation at twenty years' purchase to support his total for Britain's investment abroad. His average annual return of 5.2 per cent was copied by the Board of Trade, without acknowledgement, when the Board calculated that the capital to be derived from an overseas investment income of £210 million for 1913 must have been £4 billion.[27] If, however, the basis of the capitalisation were changed to fifteen years' purchase, in line with Giffen's own distinction between Schedules C and D and those others unincorporated in either (at roughly 50 per cent apiece), then the total would be £3.15 billion, not £4.2 billion.

This kind of calculation is in any case unrealistic, and I would not wish to put it forward myself. It may be, some day, that the rediscovery of tax records hitherto believed to have been destroyed during the Second World War, or the further development of research like Kennedy's on Scottish probates, will provide the base for the useful employment of an income tax 'method'. At present, however, that day is dauntingly remote.

## Notes

1. Paish (1909) p. 465.
2. Sir Josiah Stamp, 'The Wealth and Income of the Chief Powers', *Journal of the Royal Statistical Society*, LXXXII, IV (July 1919) pp. 448–57. Sir Josiah identifies most of the problems in his *British Incomes and Property: The Application of Official Statistics to Economic Problems* (1916) pp. 230–7.
3. *Economist* (1904), Economic and Commercial History and Review of 1903, p. 5.
4. E. Crammond, 'British Investments Abroad', *Quarterly Review*, 207 (1907) p. 246.
5. *68th Report of the Commissioners of Inland Revenue for the Year Ended 31 March 1925*: British Parliamentary Papers, 1924–5, XIV, p. 98. This

was the first report in which pre-war practice was resumed, and a similar warning was repeated annually thereafter.

6. *Report of the Commissioners of Inland Revenue on the Duties under their Management, for the Years 1856 to 1869 inclusive*: P.P. 1870, XX, p. 337.
7. This particular wording was published in P.P., 1914–16, XXIV, pp. 181–2.
8. William Sanders, 'The Income Tax System', *Financial Review of Reviews*, (March 1914) p. 276.
9. Discussion of Josiah Stamp's paper, *Journal of the Royal Statistical Society*, LXXXII, IV (July 1919) p. 495.
10. J. M. Keynes, 'Great Britain's Foreign Investments', *New Quarterly* (Feb. 1910), reported in Elizabeth Johnson (ed.), *The Collected Writings of John Maynard Keynes*, vol. XV (1971) p. 52.
11. *Report of the Departmental Committee on Income Tax*: P.P. 1905, XLIV, p. 223.
12. A. Offer, 'Empire and Social Reform: British Overseas Investment and Domestic Politics, 1908–1914', *Historical Journal*, 26, 1 (1983) p. 136.
13. Rachel R. Britton and William P. Kennedy, 'The Industrial Mobilization of Great Fortunes in Victorian Britain: The Evidence from Scottish Probate Inventories, 1876–1919', typescript 10 March 1983, p. 9.
14. *The Financial Times Income Tax Guide* (6th edn 1916) p. 18.
15. Paish (1911) p. 198.
16. A. Emil Davies, *Investments Abroad* (Chicago, 1927) pp. 64, 105–7.
17. *Economist*, 22 March 1930, p. 634.
18. Sir Robert Kindersley, 'Britain's Overseas Investments in 1933 and 1934', *Economic Journal* (Sept. 1935) p. 441. He had already claimed as much for his paper: 'British Foreign Investments in 1928', *Economic Journal* (June 1930) p. 179.
19. Sir Robert Giffen, 'Recent Accumulations of Capital in the United Kingdom', reprinted in his *Essays in Finance* (1880) p. 171. The paper was given originally to the Statistical Society on 15 January 1878; it was the first occasion on which he promoted the 'Giffen Method'.
20. 'The Investment of British Capital Abroad', *Financial Review of Reviews* (March 1906), and *Economist*, 22 Sept. 1907, p. 1537.
21. Paish (1909) p. 475.
22. Crammond, 'International Finance in Time of War', *Quarterly Review*, no. 425 (1910) pp. 318, 328.
23. *Board of Trade Journal*, CX, 29 March 1923, p. 385.
24. P. Arndt, 'Neue Beiträge sur Frage der Kapitalanlage im Ausland', *Zeitscrift für Socialwissenschaft*, N.F. VI (1915) p. 302.
25. Stamp, 'The Wealth and Income of the Chief Powers', *Journal of the Royal Statistical Society*, LXXXII (1919) p. 449.
26. Giffen's 'methodology' is explained in the second chapter ('The Valuation of 1855') in his book *The Growth of Capital* (1889) pp. 10–28. The figures for 'years purchase' in domestic investment were criticised and revised by F. W. Hirst in the amendments to his new and revised edition of G. R. Porter, *The Progress of the Nation* (1912 edn) pp. 701–2, although Hirst, presumably because it would have been

particularly troublesome to work them out again, seems to have chosen to follow the Giffen formula for British capital Schedules C and D, invested abroad.

27. *Board of Trade Journal*, CX, 29 March 1923, p. 385.

# Bibliography

## NOTE

In a book of this kind, although the secondary literature is very important (whether it supports or denies the argument), the most valuable and original material comes more often than not from the articles, news items and 'City Intelligence' columns of the daily press and the periodicals. I have drawn most particularly on the *Economist* and its offshoot the *Investor's Monthly Manual*, *The Times*, and the *Statist*. But there was a host of others, including the *Banker's Magazine*, the *Board of Trade Journal*, the *Financial News*, the *Financial Review of Reviews*, the *Financial Times* and the *Investors' Chronicle*, where foreign investment was discussed very frequently (and mostly anonymously). Some of these were indexed – rather poorly, except for *The Times* after the introduction of the Official Index in 1906, but most were not. Where I have used such material, however, it is footnoted in the text. The yearbooks of the day, the *Stock Exchange Year Book* and the *Stock Exchange Official Intelligence*, are also immensely valuable in this particular context.

Government reports (and often the minutes of evidence on which they were based) are an important source and easily procurable. I am listing some of the more obvious below, by date of publication:

*Report of the Commissioners of Inland Revenue on the Duties under their Management for the Years 1856 to 1869 inclusive*, British Parliamentary Papers (hereafter P.P.) 1870, XX.

*Annual Reports* of the Commissioners of Inland Revenue, P.P. (from 1857).

*Report of the Departmental Committee on Income Tax*, P.P. 1905, XLIV.

*Papers laid before the Imperial Conference*, 1911, P.P. 1911, X.

Minutes of Evidence, *Dominions Royal Commission*, P.P. 1914, XVII.

*Second Interim Report of the Dominions Royal Commission*, P.P. 1914, XVIII.

*Report of the Committee on Financial Facilities*, P.P. 1918, X.

*Report of the American Dollar Securities Committee*, P.P. 1919, XIII.

Minutes of Evidence, *Report of the Royal Commission on Income Tax*, P.P. 1920.

*Report of the Committee on National Debt and Taxation*, P.P. 1927, XI.

Minutes of Evidence, *Report of the Committee on Finance and Industry*, HMSO, 1931.

ADDIS, CHARLES, 'Problems of British Banking', *Edinburgh Review* (July 1918).

ADLER, DOROTHY, *British Investment in American Railways, 1834–1898* (Charlottesville, Virginia, 1970).

ADLER, J. H. (ed.), *Capital Markets and Economic Development* (New York, 1967).

ANDERSON, B. L., 'Institutional Investment Before the First World War: The Union Marine Insurance Company, 1897–1915', in Sheila Marriner (ed.), *Business and Businessmen: Studies in Business, Economic and Accounting History* (Liverpool, 1978).

ANDERSON, B. M., *Effects of the War on Money, Credit and Banking in France and the US* (New York, 1919).

ANDERSON, GORDON B., 'The Effects of the War on New Security Issues in the United States', in Patterson, *America's Changing Investment Market*.

ANON., *Records of the Glasgow Stock Exchange Association 1844–1926* (Glasgow, 1927).

ARMSTRONG, CHRISTOPHER, 'Making a Market: Selling Securities in Atlantic Canada before World War I', *Canadian Journal of Economics*, XIII, 3 (Aug. 1980).

ARNDT, H. W., *The Economic Lessons of the Nineteen Thirties* (London, 1944).

ARNDT, PAUL, 'Neue Beiträge zur Frage der Kapitalanlage im Ausland', *Zeitschrift für Socialwissenschaft*, N.F., VI (1915), article no. 3 ('Zur Statistik der Kapitalanlagen im Ausland').

ATKIN, JOHN M., 'Official Regulation of British Overseas Investment, 1914–1931', *Economic History Review*, 2s. XXIII, 2 (1970).

ATKIN, JOHN M., *British Overseas Investment, 1918–31* (New York, 1977).

BACON, NATHANIEL T., 'Capital Invested in the United States from Abroad', *Yale Review*, 9 (Nov. 1900).

BAGCHI, A. K., *Private Investment in India, 1900–1939* (Cambridge, 1972).

BAILEY, J. D., 'Australian Borrowing in Scotland in the Nineteenth Century', *Economic History Review*, 2s. XII, 2 (1959).

BALOGH, THOMAS, *Studies in Financial Organization* (Cambridge, 1947).

BARKAI, H., 'The Macro-Economics of Tsarist Russia in the Industrialisation Era: Monetary Developments, the Balance of Payments and the Gold Standard', *Journal of Economic History*, 33, 2 (June 1973).

BAXTER, R. DUDLEY, 'The Recent Progress of National Debts', *Journal of the Statistical Society*, XXXVII, I (March 1874).

BLOOMFIELD, ARTHUR I., 'The Significance of Outstanding Securities in the International Movement of Capital', *Canadian Journal of Economics and Political Science*, 6, 4 (Nov. 1940).

BLOOMFIELD, ARTHUR I., *Short-Term Capital Movements under the Pre-1914 Gold Standard* (Princeton, N.J., 1963).

BLOOMFIELD, ARTHUR I., *Patterns of Fluctuation in International Investment Before 1914* (Princeton, N.J., 1968).

BOGART, ERNEST L., *War Costs and Their Financing* (New York, 1921).

BORN, KARL E., *International Banking in the Nineteenth and Twentieth Centuries* (Leamington Spa, 1983).

BRAND, R. H., *War and National Finance* (London, 1921).

BUCKLEY, KENNETH, *Capital Formation in Canada, 1896–1930* (Toronto, 1955).

BUCKLEY, PETER J. and ROBERTS, BRIAN E., *European Direct Investment in the USA before World War I* (London, 1982).

BUTLIN, N. G., *Australian Domestic Product, Investment and Foreign Borrowing, 1861–1938/9* (Cambridge, 1962).

BUTLIN, N. G., *Investment in Australian Economic Development, 1861–1900* (Cambridge, 1964).

CAGE, R. A. (ed.), *The Scots Abroad: Labour, Capital, Enterprise, 1750–1914* (London, 1985).

CAIN, NEVILLE, 'Trade and Economic Structure at the Periphery: The Australian Balance of Payments, 1890–1965', in Colin Forster (ed.), *Australian Economic Development in the Twentieth Century* (London, 1970).

CAIN, P. J., 'J. A. Hobson, Cobdenism and the Radical Theory of Economic Imperialism, 1898–1914', *Economic History Review*, 2s. XXXI, 4 (Nov. 1978).

CAIN, P. J., 'J. A. Hobson, Finance Capitalism and Imperalism in Late Victorian and Edwardian England', *Journal of Imperial and Commonwealth History*, XIII, 3 (May 1985).

CAIRNCROSS, A. K., 'Did Foreign Investment Pay?' *Review of Economic Studies*, III (1935).

CAIRNCROSS, A. K., *Home and Foreign Investment 1870–1913: Studies in Capital Accumulation* (Cambridge, 1953).

CAROSSO, VINCENT P., *Investment Banking in America: A History* (Cambridge, Mass., 1970).

CASSEL, GUSTAV, *et al.*, *Foreign Investments* (Chicago, 1928).

CASSEL, GUSTAV, 'The Utility of Foreign Investment', in ibid.

CASSIS, Y., 'The Banking Community of London, 1890–1914: A Survey', *Journal of Imperial and Commonwealth History*, XIII, 3 (May 1985).

CECCO, MARCELLO DE, *Money and Empire: The International Gold Standard, 1890–1914* (Oxford, 1974).

CHANDAVARKAR, A. G., 'Money and Credit, 1858–1947', in Dharma Kumar (ed.), *The Cambridge Economic History of India* (Cambridge, 1983).

CHANDLER, A. D., 'The Growth of the Transnational Industrial Firm in the United States and the United Kingdom: A Comparative Analysis', *Economic History Review*, 2s. XXXIII, 3 (Aug. 1980).

CHAPMAN, STANLEY, *The Rise of Merchant Banking* (London, 1984).

CHAPMAN, STANLEY, 'British-based Investment Groups before 1914', *Economic History Review*, 2s. XXXVIII, 2 (May 1985).

CHECKLAND, S. G., 'The Mind of the City, 1870–1914', *Oxford Economic Papers*, n.s. 9, 3 (Oct. 1957).

COLE, W. A., *see* P. DEANE.

CORAM, T., 'The Role of British Capital in the Development of the United States' (unpublished M.Sc.econ. thesis, University of Southampton, 1967).

COSTIGLIOLA, FRANK C., 'Anglo-American Financial Rivalry in the 1920s', *Journal of Economic History*, XXXVII (1977).

COTTRELL, P. L., *British Overseas Investment in the Nineteenth Century* (London, 1975).

CRAMMOND, EDGAR, 'British Investment Abroad', *Quarterly Review* (July 1907).

CRAMMOND, EDGAR, 'British Investment Abroad', *Quarterly Review* (July 1911).

CRAMMOND, EDGAR, 'The Economic Position of the Allied Powers', *Quarterly Review* (July 1915).

CURRIE, A. W., 'British Attitudes Toward Investment in North American Railroads', *Business History Review*, 34, 2 (Summer 1960).

DAVIES, A. EMIL, *The Money and the Stock and Share Markets* (London, 1926).

DAVIES, A. EMIL, *Investments Abroad* (Chicago, 1927).

DAVIES, ERNST, 'Foreign Investment', in G. D. H. Cole (ed.), *Studies in Capital and Investment* (London, 1935).

DAVIS, LANCE E. and HUTTENBACK, ROBERT A., 'The Political Economy of British Imperialism: Measures of Benefit and Support', *Journal of Economic History*, XLII, 1 (March 1982).

DAVIS, LANCE E., 'The Export of British Finance, 1865–1914', *Journal of Imperial and Commonwealth History*, XIII, 3 (May 1985).

DEANE, P. and COLE, W. A., *British Economic Growth, 1688–1959* (Cambridge, 1964).

DRUMMOND, I. M., 'Capital Markets in Australia and Canada, 1895–1914' (unpublished Ph.D. thesis, Yale, 1959).

DRUMMOND, I. M., 'Government Securities on Colonial New Issue Markets: Australia and Canada, 1895–1914', *Yale Economic Essays*, I, 1 (Spring 1961).

DRUMMOND, I. M., 'Canadian Life Insurance Companies and the Capital Market, 1890–1914', *Canadian Journal of Economics and Political Science*, 28, 2 (May 1962).

DUCRUET, JEAN, *Les Capitaux Européens au Proche-Orient* (Paris, 1964).

DUGUID, CHARLES, *The Story of the Stock Exchange* (London, 1901).

DUNNING, JOHN H., *Studies in International Investment* (London, 1970).

ECONOMIC COMMISSION FOR LATIN AMERICA (ECLA), *External Financing in Latin America* (New York, 1965).

EDELSTEIN, MICHAEL, 'The Rate of Return on UK Home and Foreign Investment, 1870–1913' (unpublished Ph.D. thesis, University of Pennysylvania, 1970).

EDELSTEIN, MICHAEL, 'The Determinants of UK Investment Abroad, 1870–1913: The US Case', *Journal of Economic History*, XXXIV, 4 (Dec. 1974).

EDELSTEIN, MICHAEL, 'Realized Rates of Return on UK Home and Overseas Portfolio Investment in the Age of High Imperialism', *Explorations in Economic History*, 13 (1976).

EDELSTEIN, MICHAEL, 'Foreign Investment and Empire, 1860–1914', in Roderick Floud and Ronald McCloskey (eds), *The Economic History of Britain Since 1700*, vol. 2 (Cambridge, 1981).

EDELSTEIN, MICHAEL, *Overseas Investment in the Age of High Imperialism: The United Kingdom, 1850–1914* (New York, 1982).

FEINSTEIN, CHARLES H., *National Income, Expenditure and Output of the United Kingdom, 1855–1965* (Cambridge, 1971).

FEINSTEIN, CHARLES H. (1982), *see under* R. C. O. Matthews.

FEIS, HERBERT, *Europe the World's Banker* (New Haven, Conn., 1930).

FIELDHOUSE, D. K., *Unilever Overseas: The Anatomy of a Multi-National, 1895–1965* (London, 1978).

FINANCIAL TIMES, *Investors' Guide* (London, 1913, new edn 1923).

FISK, HARVEY E., *The Inter-Ally Debts: An Analysis of War and Post-War Public Finance, 1914–23* (New York, 1924).

FLUX, A. W., 'The Yield on High-Class Investments, 1896–1910', *Transactions of the Manchester Statistical Society* (Feb. 1911).

FORD, A. G., 'The Transfer of British Foreign Lending, 1870–1913', *Economic History Review*, 2s. XI, 2 (1958).

FORD, A. G., *The Gold Standard, 1880–1914: Britain and Argentina* (Oxford, 1962).

FORD, A. G., 'British Economic Fluctuations, 1870–1914', *Manchester School*, XXXVII (1969).

FORD, A. G., 'British Investment in Argentina and Long Swings, 1880–1914', *Journal of Economic History*, XXXI, 3 (Sept. 1971).

FOXWELL, H. S., 'British War Finance', *Economic Journal* (Dec. 1915).

FOXWELL, H. S., *Papers on Current Finance* (London, 1919).

FRANKEL, S. H., 'Return to Capital in the Witwatersrand Gold Industry, 1887–1932', *Economic Journal*, XLV (1935).

FRANKEL, S. H., *Capital Investment in Africa: Its Cause and Effects* (London, 1938).

FRASER, J. B., 'The Emigration of Capital', *Contemporary Review* (April 1904).

GENERAL SECURITIES CORPORATION, *The Investor's Handy Book of Active Stocks and Shares* (London, 1913).

GIBSON, A. H., 'Banking, Currency, War Finance, etc.', in Adam W. Kirkaldy (ed.), *Industry and Finance* (London, 1920).

GIFFEN, ROBERT, *Essays in Finance* (London, 1880).

GIFFEN, ROBERT, *The Growth of Capital* (London, 1889).

GIFFEN, ROBERT, 'The Expenditure of National Capital', *Journal of the Institute of Bankers*, XXII, VI (June 1901).

GIFFEN, ROBERT, 'Notes on Imports Versus Home Production and Home Versus Foreign Investments', *Economic Journal*, XV (Dec. 1905).

GILBERT, J. C., *A History of Investment Trusts in Dundee, 1873–1938* (London, 1939).

GILLE, BERTRAND, *Les Investissements Français en Italie, 1815–1914* (Turin, 1968).

GIRAULT, RENÉ, *Emprunts Russes et Investissements Français en Russie, 1887–1914* (Paris, 1973).

GLASGOW, GEORGE, *The Scottish Investment Trust Companies* (London, 1932).

GRANT, A. T. K., *A Study of the Capital Market in Britain from 1919–1936* (London, 1937).

GREEN, ALAN and URQUHART, M. C., 'Factors and Commodity Flows in the International Economy of 1870–1914: A Multi-Country View', *Journal of Economic History*, 36 (1976).

GREGORY, P. R., 'The Russian Balance of Payments, the Gold Standard, and Monetary Policy: A Historical Example of Foreign Capital Movements', *Journal of Economic History*, 39 (1979).

GREGORY, THEODOR E., 'Foreign Investments and British Public Opinion', in Cassel, *Foreign Investments*.

GUYOT, YVES, 'The Amount, Direction and Nature of French Investments', in Patterson, *America's Changing Investment Market*.

HALL, A. R., 'A Note on the English Capital Market as a Source for Home Investment before 1914', *Economica*, n.s. XXIV (Feb. 1957).

HALL, A. R., *The London Capital Market and Australia, 1870–1914* (Canberra, 1963).

HALL, A. R. (ed.), *The Export of Capital from Britain 1870–1914* (London, 1968).

HALL, A. R., *The Stock Exchange of Melbourne and the Victorian Economy, 1852–1900* (Canberra, 1968).

HARTLAND, PENELOPE, 'Private Enterprise and International Capital', *Canadian Journal of Economics and Political Science*, XIX, I (Feb. 1953).

HARTLAND, PENELOPE, 'Canada's Balance of Payments since 1868', in National Bureau of Economic Research, *Trends in the American Economy in the Nineteenth Century* (Princeton, N.J., 1960).

HIRST, F. W., *British Capital at Home and Abroad: An Examination of Recent Statements as to Exports of Capital Abroad* (London, 1910).

HIRST, F. W., *The Credit of Nations, with Special Reference to the Debts of Great Britain, Germany, France and the United States* (Washington, D.C., 1910).

HIRST, F. W., *The Stock Exchange: A Short Study of Investment and Speculation* (London, 1911).

HIRST, F. W. and LAYTON, W. T., 'The Growth of Wealth and Capital', in G. R. Porter, *The Progress of the Nation* (London, 1912 edn).

HOBSON, C. K., *Export of Capital* (London, 1914).

HOBSON, C. K., 'British Overseas Investments, Their Growth and Importance', *Annals of the American Academy of Political and Social Science*, LXVIII (Nov. 1916).

HOBSON, C. K., 'The Amount, Direction and Nature of French Investments', in ibid.

HOBSON, C. K., 'British Overseas Investments; Their Growth and Importance', in Patterson, *America's Changing Investment Market*.

HOBSON, J. A., 'The Economic Taproot of Imperialism', *Contemporary Review* (Aug. 1902).

HOBSON, J. A., *An Economic Interpretation of Investment* (London, 1911).

HOLMES, GEORGE J., *The Investors' Bluebook for 1914* (London, 1914).

HOU, CHI-MING, *Foreign Investment and Economic Development in China, 1840–1937* (Cambridge, Mass., 1965).

HUEBNER, S. S., 'The American Security Market During the War', in Patterson, *America's Changing Investment Market*.

HUTTENBACK, ROBERT A., *see under* Lance E. Davis.

IMLAH, ALBERT H., 'British Balance of Payments and Export of Capital, 1816–1913', *Economic History Review*, 2s. V, 2 (1952).

IMLAH, ALBERT H., *Economic Elements in the Pax Britannica: Studies in British Foreign Trade in the Nineteenth Century* (Cambridge, Mass., 1958).

JAGTIANI, H. M., *The Role of the State in the Provision of Railways* (London, 1924).

JENKS, LELAND H., *The Migration of British Capital to 1875* (New York, 1927).

JENKS, LELAND H., 'British Experience with Foreign Investments', *Journal of Economic History*, 4, Supplement (Dec. 1944).

JENKS, LELAND H., 'Britain and American Railway Development', *Journal of Economic History*, XI, 4 (1951).

JONES, CHARLES, 'Great Capitalists and the Direction of British Overseas Investment in the late Nineteenth Century: The Case of Argentina', *Business History*, XXII, 2 (July 1980).

JOHNSON, E. (ed.), *The Collected Writings of John Maynard Keynes*, vol. XV (London, 1971).

KENNEDY, W. P., 'Foreign Investment, Trade and Growth in the UK, 1870–1914', *Explorations in Economic History*, 11, 4 (Summer 1974).

KENNEDY, W. P., 'Institutional Response to Economic Growth: Capital Markets in Britain to 1914', in Leslie Hannah (ed.), *Management Strategy and Business Development; An Historical and Comparative Study* (London, 1976).

KENNEDY, W. P., 'Notes on Economic Efficiency in Historical Perspective: The Case of Britain, 1870–1914', *Research in Economic History*, 9 (1984).

KERR, E. G., *Scottish Capital on the American Credit Frontier* (Austin, Texas, 1976).

KEYNES, J. M., 'Great Britain's Foreign Investments', *New Quarterly* (Feb. 1910).

KEYNES, J. M., 'Foreign Investment and National Advantage', *The Nation and the Athenaeum*, 9 Aug. 1924.

KEYNES, J. M., see E. Johnson.

KINDERSLEY, ROBERT, 'A New Study of British Foreign Investments', *Economic Journal*, 39 (March 1929).

KINDERSLEY, ROBERT, 'British Foreign Investments in 1928', *Economic Journal*, 40 (June 1930).

KINDERSLEY, ROBERT, 'British Foreign Investments in 1929', *Economic Journal*, 41 (Sept. 1931).

KINDERSLEY, ROBERT, 'British Foreign Investments in 1930', *Economic Journal*, 42 (June 1932).

KINDERSLEY, ROBERT, 'British Overseas Investments in 1931', *Economic Journal*, 43 (June 1933).

KINDERSLEY, ROBERT 'British Overseas Investments in 1932 and 1933', *Economic Journal*, 44 (Sept. 1934).

KINDERSLEY, ROBERT, 'Britain's Oversea Investments in 1933 and 1934', *Economic Journal*, 45 (Sept. 1935).
KINDERSLEY, ROBERT, 'Britain's Overseas Investments in 1934 and 1935', *Economic Journal*, 46 (Dec. 1936).
KINDERSLEY, ROBERT, 'British Overseas Investments in 1935 and 1936', *Economic Journal*, 47 (Dec. 1937).
KINDERSLEY, ROBERT, 'British Overseas Investments, 1937', *Economic Journal*, 48 (Dec. 1938).
KINDERSLEY, ROBERT, 'British Oversea Investments, 1938', *Economic Journal*, 49 (Dec. 1939).
KINDLEBERGER, CHARLES P., *International Short-Term Capital Movements* (New York, 1937).
KINDLEBERGER, CHARLES P., *Economic Growth in France and Britain, 1851–1950* (Cambridge, Mass., 1964).
KINDLEBERGER, CHARLES P., *A Financial History of Western Europe* (London, 1984).
KING, W. T. C., *History of the London Discount Market* (London, 1936).
KIRKALDY, A. W. (ed.), *British Finance During and After the War 1914–1921* (London, 1921).
KNAPP, JOHN, 'Capital Exports and Growth', *Economic Journal* (Sept. 1957).
KNOX, FRANK A., 'Excursus on Canadian Capital Movements and Canadian Balance of International Payments, 1900–1934', in Herbert Marshall *et al.*, *Canadian-American Industry: A Study in International Investment* (New Haven, Conn., 1936).
KUBICEK, ROBERT, 'Finance Capital and South African Goldmining 1886–1914', *Journal of Imperial and Commonwealth History*, III, 3 (1975).
KUBICEK, ROBERT, *Economic Imperialism in Theory and Practice. The Case of South African Gold Mining Finance, 1886–1914* (Durham, N.C., 1979).
KUZNETS, SIMON, *Capital in the American Economy: Its Formation and Financing* (Princeton, N.J., 1961).
LAVINGTON, F., *The English Capital Market* (London, 1921).
LAWSON, W. R., *The Scottish Investors' Manual: A Review of Leading Scottish Securities in 1883* (Edinburgh, 1884).
LAWSON, W. R., *British War Finance, 1914–15* (London, 1915).
LAWSON, W. R. 'The British Treasury and the London Stock Exchange', in Patterson, *America's Changing Investment Market*.
LAYTON, W. T., *see* F. W. Hirst (1912).
LEAGUE OF NATIONS. *The Course and Phases of the World Economic Depression* (Geneva, 1931).
LEHFELDT, R. A., 'The Rate of Interest on British and Foreign Investments', *Journal of the Royal Statistical Society*, LXXVI (Jan. and March 1913).
LEHFELDT, R. A., 'The Rate of Interest on British and Foreign Investments', *Journal of the Royal Statistical Society*, LXXVII, IV (1914).
LEHFELDT, R. A. 'The Rate of Interest on British and Foreign Investments', *Journal of the Royal Statistical Society*, LXXVIII (1915).

LENFANT, J. H., 'British Capital Export, 1900–1913 (unpublished Ph.D. thesis, University of London, 1949).

LENFANT, J. H., 'Great Britain's Capital Formation, 1865–1914', *Economica*, new ser. XVIII (1951).

LEVY-LEBOYER, MAURICE, 'La Capacité Financière de la France au Debut du XXe Siècle', in idem (ed.), *La Position Internationale de la France: Aspects Économiques et Financiers XIXe–XXe Siècles* (Paris, 1977).

LEWIS, CLEONA, *The International Accounts* (New York, 1927).

LEWIS, CLEONA, *America's Stake in International Investments* (Washington, 1938).

LEWIS, COLIN M., *British Railways in Argentina 1857–1914: A Case Study of Foreign Investment* (London, 1983).

LOWENFELD, HENRY, *All About Investment* (London, 1909).

MACKENZIE, J. A. P., 'Investments of French Capital Abroad', *Journal of the Royal Statistical Society*, LXVI (Dec. 1903).

MARSHALL, HERBERT, *et al.*, *Canadian-American Industry: A Study in International Investment* (New Haven, Conn., 1936).

MARWICK, W. H., 'Scottish Overseas Investment in the Nineteenth Century', *Scottish Bankers' Magazine*, 27 (July 1935).

MATTHEWS, R. C. O., FEINSTEIN, C. H. and ODLING-SMEE, J. C. *British Economic Growth 1856–1973* (Oxford, 1982).

MEIER, G. M., 'Economic Development and the Transfer Mechanism, Canada, 1895–1913', *Canadian Journal of Economics and Political Science*, XIX, 1 (Feb. 1953).

MICHIE, R. C., 'Options, Concessions, Syndicates, and the Provision of Venture Capital, 1880–1913', *Business History*, XXIII, 2 (July 1981).

MICHIE, R. C. *Money, Mania and Markets: Investment, Company Formation and the Stock Exchange in Nineteenth Century Scotland* (Edinburgh, 1981).

MICHIE, R. C. *Money, Mania and Markets: Investment, Company Formation and the Stock Exchange in Nineteenth Century Scotland* 1983).

MICHIE, R. C., 'The London Stock Exchange and the British Securities Market, 1850–1914', *Economic History Review*, 2s. XXXVIII, 1 (1985).

MICHIE, R. C., 'The London and New York Stock Exchanges, 1850–1914', forthcoming.

MITCHELL, B. R., *Abstract of British Historical Statistics* (Cambridge, 1962).

MITCHELL, B. R., *European Historical Statistics, 1750–1970* (London, 1975).

MORGAN, E. V., *Studies in British Financial Policy, 1914–25* (London, 1952).

MORGAN, E. V. and THOMAS, W. A., *The Stock Exchange: Its History and Functions* (London, 1962).

MORGENSTERN, OSCAR, *International Financial Transactions and Business Cycles* (Princeton, N.J., 1959).

MYERS, MARGARET, *The New York Money Market: Origins and Development* (New York, 1931).

MYERS, MARGARET, *Paris as a Financial Centre* (London, 1936).
NASH, ROBERT L., *A Short Inquiry into the Profitable Nature of Our Investments* (London, 1881).
NICHOLAS, S. J., 'British Multinational Investment before 1939', *Journal of European Economic History*, 11, 3 (Winter 1982).
NOYES, ALEXANDER D., *Forty Years of American Finance* (New York, 1909).
NOYES, ALEXANDER D., *Financial Chapters of the War* (London, 1916).
NOYES, ALEXANDER D., *The War Period of American Finance, 1908–1925* (New York, 1926).
NURKSE, RAGNAR, 'International Investment Today in the Light of Nineteenth Century Experience', *Economic Journal*, LXIX (Dec. 1954).
ODLING-SMEE, J. C., *see* R. C. O. Matthews.
OFFER, AVNER, 'Empire and Social Reform: British Overseas Investment and Domestic Politics, 1908–1914', *Historical Journal*, 26, 1 (1983).
O'HAGAN, H. OSBORNE, *Leaves from my Life* (London, 1929).
PAISH, F. W., 'The London New Issue Market', *Economica*, new ser. XVIII, 69 (1951).
PAISH, GEORGE, 'Great Britain's Capital Investments in Other Lands', *Journal of the Royal Statistical Society*, LXXII, III (Sept. 1909).
PAISH, GEORGE, 'Great Britain's Capital Investments in Individual Colonies and Foreign Countries', *Journal of the Royal Statistical Society*, LXXIV, II (Jan. 1911).
PAISH, GEORGE, 'The Export of Capital and the Cost of Living', *Statist* (Supplement), 14 Feb. 1914.
PAISH, GEORGE, 'War Finance', *Journal of the Royal Statistical Society*, LXXXIX, III (May 1916).
PANDIT, Y. S., *India's Balance of Indebtedness, 1898–1913* (London, 1937).
PATERSON, D. G., *British Direct Investment in Canada, 1890–1914* (Toronto, 1976).
PATTERSON, E. L. S., 'London and New York as Financial Centers', in Patterson, *America's Changing Investment Market*.
PATTERSON, E. M. (ed.), *America's Changing Investment Market* (Philadelphia, 1916).
PETERS, HAROLD E., *The Foreign Debt of the Argentine Republic* (Baltimore, 1934).
PHELPS, VERNON L., *The International Position of Argentina* (Philadelphia, 1938).
PLATT, D. C. M., 'British Portfolio Investment Overseas before 1870: Some Doubts', *Economic History Review*, 2s. XXXIII, 1 (Feb. 1980).
PLATT, D. C. M., 'Financing the Expansion of Cities, 1860–1914', *Urban History Review*, XI, 3 (Feb. 1983).
PLATT, D. C. M., *Foreign Finance in Continental Europe and the USA 1815–1870: Quantities, Origins, Functions & Distribution* (London, 1984).
PLATT, D. C. M., 'The Financing of City Expansion: Buenos Aires and Montreal Compared, 1880–1914', in D. C. M. Platt and Guido di Tella

(eds), *Argentina, Australia and Canada: Studies in Comparative Development, 1870–1965* (London, 1985).

PLATT, D. C. M. 'Canada and Argentina: The First Preference of the British Investor, 1904–14', *Journal of Imperial and Commonwealth History*, XIII, 3 (May 1985).

PLATT, D. C. M. 'Domestic Finance in the Growth of Buenos Aires, 1880–1914', in Guido di Tella and D. C. M. Platt (eds), *The Political Economy of Argentina, 1880–1946* (London, 1986).

POLLARD, SYDNEY, 'Capital Exports, 1870–1914: Harmful or Beneficial?', *Economic History Review*, 2s. XXXVIII, 4 (1985).

POWELL, ELLIS T., *The Mechanism of the City* (London, 1910).

POWELL, ELLIS T., *The Evolution of the Money Market, 1885–1915* (London, 1915).

REMER, C. F., *Foreign Investments in China* (New York, 1933).

RICHARDSON, H. W., 'British Emigration and Overseas Investment, 1870–1914', *Economic History Review*, 2s. XXV, 1 (Feb. 1972).

RIPPY, J. F., 'British Investments in Latin America and India', *Inter American Economic Affairs*, VII (1953–4).

RIPPY, J. F., *British Investments in Latin America 1822–1949* (Minneapolis, 1959).

ROBERTS, BRIAN R., *see* Peter J. Buckley.

ROSENBERG, W., 'Capital Imports and Growth – the Case of New Zealand: Foreign Investment in New Zealand, 1840–1958', *Economic Journal*, 71 (1961).

ROYAL INSTITUTE OF INTERNATIONAL AFFAIRS (CHATHAM HOUSE), *The Problem of International Investment* (London, 1937).

ROZENRAAD, CORNELIUS, 'The International Money Market', *Journal of the Royal Statistical Society*, LXIII, I (March 1900).

RUBINSTEIN, W. D., *Men of Property: The Very Wealthy in Britain since the Industrial Revolution* (London, 1981).

SALTER, ARTHUR, *Foreign Investment* (Essays in Finance, No. 12, Princeton, N.J., 1951).

SAMUEL, ARTHUR M., 'Has Foreign Investment Paid?' *Economic Journal*, 40 (March 1930).

SCHUSTER, FELIX, 'Foreign Trade and the Money Market', *Journal of the Institute of Bankers*, XXV, II (Feb. 1904).

SEGAL, HARVEY and SIMON, MATTHEW, 'British Foreign Capital Issues, 1865–1894', *Journal of Economic History*, 21, 4 (Dec. 1961).

SHEPPARD, DAVID K., *The Growth and Role of UK Financial Institutions, 1880–1962* (London, 1971).

SIMKIN, C. G. F., *The Instability of a Dependent Economy: Economic Fluctuations in New Zealand, 1840–1914* (Oxford, 1951).

SIMON, MATTHEW, 'The United States Balance of Payments, 1861–1900', in National Bureau of Economic Research, *Trends in the American Economy in the Nineteenth Century* (Princeton, N.J., 1960).

SIMON, MATTHEW, *see* Harvey Segal (1961).

SIMON, MATTHEW, 'The Enterprise and Industrial Composition of New British Portfolio Foreign Investment, 1865–1914', *Journal of Development Studies*, 3, 3 (April 1967).

SIMON, MATTHEW, 'The Pattern of New British Portfolio Investment, 1865–1914', in Adler, *Capital Markets*.

SIMON, MATTHEW, 'New British Investment in Canada, 1865–1914', *Canadian Journal of Economics*, 3, 2 (1970).

SKINNER, THOMAS (ed.), *The Stock Exchange Year Book* (London, annually from 1875).

SOBEL, ROBERT, *The Big Board: A History of the New York Stock Market* (New York, 1965).

SOBEL, ROBERT, *The Great Bull Market: Wall Street in the 1920s* (New York, 1968).

SONNE, H. C., *The City: Its Finance July 1914 to July 1915 and Future* (London, 1915).

SPALDING, W. F., 'The Foreign Branch Banks in England and Their Influence on the London Money Market', *Economic Journal* (Dec. 1912).

SPENCE, CLARK C., *British Investments and the American Mining Frontier, 1860–1901* (New York, 1958).

STALEY, E., *War and the Private Investor: A Study in the Relations of International Politics and International Private Investment* (Chicago, 1935).

STAMP, JOSIAH, *British Incomes and Property: The Application of Official Statistics to Economic Problems* (1916).

STAMP, JOSIAH, 'The Wealth and Income of the Chief Powers', *Journal of the Royal Statistical Society*, LXXXII, IV (July 1919).

STAMP, JOSIAH, *The National Income 1924* (Oxford, 1927).

STILLSON, RICHARD T., 'The Financing of Malayan Rubber, 1905–1923', *Economic History Review*, 2s. XXIV, 4 (1971).

STOCKBROKER, A., 'The Depreciation of British Home Investments', *Economic Journal*, XXII, 86 (June 1912); *see also Economic Journal* (June 1913) and (June 1914).

STONE, IRVING, 'British Long-Term Investment in Latin America, 1865–1913', *Business History Review* (1968).

STONE, IRVING, 'British Investment in Argentina', *Journal of Economic History*, XXXII, 2 (June 1972).

STONE, IRVING, 'British Direct and Portfolio Investment in Latin America before 1914', *Journal of Economic History*, XXXVII, 3 (Sept. 1977).

STONE, J. M., 'Financial Panics: Their Implications for the Mix of Domestic and Foreign Investments in Great Britain, 1880–1913', *Quarterly Journal of Economics*, LXXV (1971).

STOPFORD, J., 'The Origins of British Based Multinational Manufacturing Enterprises', *Business History Review*, XLVIII, 3 (Autumn 1974).

STOVEL, JOHN A., *Canada in the World Economy* (Cambridge, Mass., 1959).

SUN, E-TU ZEN, *Chinese Railways and British Interests* (New York, 1954).

SUPPLE, BARRY, *The Royal Exchange Assurance. A History of British Assurance 1720–1970* (Cambridge, 1970).

SVEDBERG, PETER, 'The Portfolio: Direct Composition of Private Foreign Investment in 1914 Revisited', *Economic Journal*, 88 (1978).

SYKES, E. W., 'The Growth of London as the Financial Centre of the World', *Journal of the Institute of Bankers*, 32 (1902).

THANE, PAT, 'Financiers and the British State 1880–1914: The Case of Sir Ernest Cassel', unpublished discussion paper, Institute of Commonwealth Studies, University of London, June 1985.
THOMAS, BRINLEY, 'The Historical Record of International Capital Movements to 1913', in Adler, *Capital Movements*.
THOMAS, W. A., *see* E. V. Morgan (1962).
THOMAS, W. A., *The Provincial Stock Exchanges* (London, 1973).
TREBLE, J. H., 'The Pattern of Investment of the Standard Life Assurance Company 1875–1914', *Business History*, XXII, 2 (July 1980).
UNITED NATIONS, *International Capital Movements during the Inter-War Period* (New York, 1949).
UNITED NATIONS, Department of Economic and Social Affairs, 'The Growth of Foreign Investments in Latin America', reproduced in Marvin D. Bernstein (comp. and ed.), *Foreign Investment in Latin America* (New York, 1966).
URQUHART, M. C., *see under* Alan Green.
VINER, JACOB, *Canada's Balance of International Indebtedness 1900–1913* (Cambridge, Mass., 1924).
WHEELER, J. F., *The Stock Exchange* (London, n.d. probably 1913).
WHITE, HARRY D., *French International Accounts, 1880–1913* (Cambridge, Mass., 1933).
WILKINS, MIRA, *The Emergence of Multinational Enterprise: American Business Abroad from the Colonial Era to 1914* (Cambridge, Mass., 1970).
WILKINS, MIRA, *The Maturing of Multinational Enterprise* (Cambridge, Mass., 1976).
WILKINS, MIRA (comp. and ed.), *British Overseas Investments, 1907–1948* (New York, 1977).
WILKINS, MIRA, 'Modern European Economic History and the Multinationals', *Journal of European History*, 6, 3 (Winter 1977).
WILKINS, MIRA, 'The History of European Multinationals – A New Look', forthcoming.
WILLIAMS, DAVID, 'London and the 1931 Financial Crisis', *Economic History Review*, 2s. XV, 3 (1963).
WILLIAMS-TAYLOR, FREDERICK, 'Canadian Loans in London', *United Empire*, n.s. III (Dec. 1912).
WILSON, RONALD, *Capital Imports and the Terms of Trade* (Melbourne, 1931).
WITHERS, HARTLEY, *Stocks and Shares* (London, 1910).
WITHERS, HARTLEY, *War and Lombard Street* (London, 1915).
WITHERS, HARTLEY, *International Finance* (London, 1916).
WOOD, GORDON, *Borrowings and Business in Australia: A Study of the Correlation between Imports and Capital and Changes in National Prosperity* (London, 1930).
WOODRUFF, WILLIAM, *Impact of Western Man: A Study of Europe's Role in the World Economy, 1750–1960* (New York, 1966).
WOODRUFF, WILLIAM, *America's Impact on the World* (London, 1975).
WYSE, R. C., 'Future of London as the World's Money Market', *Economic Journal* (Dec. 1918).

# Index